Aimee

May God remain near
in your life

Jack Ream

When God Acts

Jack Ream

PublishAmerica
Baltimore

PublishAmerica has allowed this work to remain exactly as the author intended, verbatim, without editorial input.

Hardcover 978-1-4560-3404-7
Softcover 978-1-4560-3405-4
PUBLISHED BY PUBLISHAMERICA, LLLP
www.publishamerica.com
Baltimore

Printed in the United States of America

Introduction

For most of my life I had the typical attitude toward poverty; poverty was due to the irresponsibility of those who had the problem. On the surface this appears to be the case and if you haven't personally experienced poverty all you have to go on is appearances. Since I believed this to be the case, I felt no responsibility to do anything about any of the poverty problems facing our world today—especially hunger and homelessness. Unfortunately, this attitude is a gross misunderstanding of the problem and, if you claim to be a Christian, it is also a gross misunderstanding of what Jesus stood for.

All of my life I have claimed to be a Christian and even though there are many places in scripture where we are called upon to take the poor and oppressed into our consideration, I didn't take any of them seriously mainly because the church didn't seem to take them seriously. As a teenager, the hypocrisy of the church was troubling to me, but life presented enough other problems, that it remained troubling, but no more. Pastors talked about helping the poor but I didn't see many people doing anything to alleviate the conditions in an organized way. The church in the United States found it very convenient to turn the problem over to the federal and state governments. The government had the money; surely they could do something to alleviate the situation. A few churches set up organizations that served the poor, but for the most part, they haven't called on their own membership to become involved. Hired staff runs these organizations. Most of the people in the pews are not involved in the efforts. As time passed and I gained education, the hypocrisy of the church became a serious issue with me, but I felt that there was nothing I could do about it—one person against an institution. I had more important things to concentrate on, so I dropped out of church. It is not surprising that the church has done very little. The church is you and I, and if most people have the attitude toward poverty that I have had most of my life, and many do, it is understandable that the church has done very little.

God has always called on those who believe in him to take responsibility for those in poverty. The prophets of the Hebrew Scriptures, speaking for God severely criticized both the leadership and the people for not taking care of their poor and oppressed. For over 200 years they criticized, and the people ignored them. The prophets continually told them that if they didn't change, they would loose their country. In the 6th century, BCE, they were conquered.

Almost 2000 years ago, Jesus told us that the poor would be with us always, and again warned us that we should take care of them. In fact in the 25th chapter of Matthew, he warns us what will happen in the long run unless we take care of the poor and oppressed. Still the church has historically to a great extent ignored the problem. I think the church's idea of justice and God's idea of justice are not even close to being the same. 2000 years have been spent concentrating on morality, sin and control of people's behavior, without substantially improving morality or reducing sin, and doing very little to reduce poverty. There is evidence that the early church, while they were oppressed by the Roman Empire, did take care of the poor. But since the 4th century the church has been on the side of the oppressor and has largely ignored the poor.

My attitude toward poverty, however, changed several years ago when God got my attention. When you know that God has visited you, your whole understanding of who God is and how God operates is suddenly and dramatically changed. Until that visit God was not real to me; he was just an idea. I now know how serious God is about justice and compassion. **Over night**, God changed my attitude, and my life. I am sure that the changes have made me a better person. I can now understand what happened to Saul of Tarsus on the road to Damascus and as a result, can better understand his letters to the churches. Life has become exciting for me in my senior years. Now, some of those same life-changing experiences are happening in those who are working with me on various ecumenical projects to reduce the effects of poverty. Words are not adequate to describe what I have experienced; therefore, I am going to tell you a story. It is the story of the changes that have taken place to affect my life, the life of the congregation of the church that I attend, and the life of the community in which all of this took place. It is also a story about God, how I see him trying to communicates with mankind, and what Happens when God acts..

Most people whom I know seldom, if ever, experience God in their lives simply because they do not see what God is doing in their life. God tries to direct our lives but my experience tells me that most of the time we aren't paying attention. I hope this book will help change your image and understanding of God, and will give you some reasons to begin looking at what God is doing.

Let me say at the very beginning that the statements made about God in this story are strictly my opinion and have come through my experiences with life—its problems and pleasures, as well as my experience of God. They do not represent the belief or practices of any organized church that I know of. I believe that God tries to communicate with people. I know that God has communicated with me on many occasions. The Holy Spirit is as real as I am and I try hard to follow what the Spirit tells me to do. I offer no proof that God is real, but this book should tell you why I believe that this is so, and the benefits to you of letting God direct your life.

Chapter 1
The Open Door

Then the word of the Lord came to him, saying,
"What are you doing here, Elijah?"
He answered, "I have been very zealous for the Lord, the
God of hosts;"——
He said, "Go out and stand on the mountain before the Lord,
for the Lord is about to pass by."
Now there was a great wind, so strong that it was splintering
the mountains
    and breaking rocks in pieces before the Lord,
    but the Lord was not in the wind;
    and after the wind an earthquake,
    but the Lord was not in the earthquake;
    and after the earthquake a fire,
    but the Lord was not in the fire;
    and after the fire a sound of sheer silence.
    When Elijah heard it, he wrapped his face in his mantle
    And went out and stood at the entrance to the cave.
    Then there came a voice to him...
    I Kings 19:9-13
This story is about a small Episcopal Church in the midwest
and how God changed the mission of the church and the lives
of the people in the congregation. During the narrative of this
story I will refer to the church as "the parish". The things that

have occurred were not the result of a plan, at least not a plan of the congregation; you might say they just happened That's what most people say in situations like that, "We didn't plan it that way, it just happened." If you look closely at the things that 'just happen' you will find God's action in there somewhere. In this case, I think God was trying to get the attention of the members of this parish and I will point out, as the story goes along, where I think God was behind what happened. The parish members were not interested in change so they were not expecting God to intervene in their lives. They enjoyed the status quo and would have been happy to maintain it. The parish could be any church in any town; its uniqueness is due to the way it responded to circumstances.

In the 1990's the parish had about 100 members and an average Sunday attendance of between 30 and 50. As any church organization, the congregation was very hospitable and generous. There were about 40 contributing families in the parish, and its size had been fairly constant for many years. With an annual budget of between $60,000 and $70,000 per year they couldn't afford a full time priest. Like many struggling parishes the average age of its members was probably in the 50's. Life was good for the members of this congregation, so they saw no reason to change. While it was obvious that the parish had to attract some new members, no one was in a hurry to get that done. They looked at evangelism as a dirty word, as do most churches with an aging population. The parish received very little help or attention from its diocesan officials. Most church-growth people would probably have classified this as a dying parish, or at least one that would need a lot of help in the near future if it were to survive.

There had not been an adult Sunday school class in the parish for years until recently. When life is satisfactory the way it is, why spend the time finding out how it can be better? Besides, the congregation knew how they were supposed to behave. They were aware of all the cultural mores and customs. Individually they didn't feel that they needed any further education, so the adult Sunday school class wasn't very well attended.

All these facts are important to the story because they describe an average, struggling, small parish with very limited resources; a parish, like so many other small parishes with an aging population, that was so self satisfied that it did not want to put forth the effort necessary to make the church grow. It did not recognize that the church is essentially an educational organization, mainly in the business of educating itself and its members. The energy level of the parish was very low. They chose not to exert the energy to provide for the future welfare of the parish; after all, life was comfortable as it was. Why risk the troubles that come with change?

In retrospect, I can now see that God was not satisfied with the way things were going in this parish. My connection to the parish was somewhat puzzling to me. I am native to the community in which the parish is located, but my career had taken me to another community about 35 miles south on the interstate highway. After years of absence, I felt the need to return to the parish that had nurtured me and brought me back to the church. In a way, I felt that I was sent back, but I had no idea why. I was about to find out why. Because I felt that somehow I was sent back to the parish, I also felt a strong need to be active in the church and give leadership where I could, so I was a part of the Sunday school, was on the vestry of the parish, and participated in as many activities of the parish as I could. I frequently had ideas related to making the church grow, but had not been able to get other members of the parish interested in putting them into practice.

Looking back at the events of the last 15 years, I conclude that God decided that it was time for the parish to change, to view life from a different perspective. This book will explain how and why I have come to that conclusion. The events that were to successfully bring about the change in the parish started with a discussion about the locked front doors of the churches in the town, and particularly the front door of the parish church. In 1995 the vestry pondered the question of unlocking the front door. As with most questions that become an issue there were two sides to this one. Those who were concerned about personal safety and the integrity of the building took the dominant position. The societal upheaval of the 1960's and 70's had awakened everyone to the fact that not all members of society respected the sanctity of the church, so, like a turtle when threatened, they withdrew into their shell. The churches became more like closed communities. The doors were locked for safety. The historical and traditional openness of the church was abandoned. On the other side of the question were those who felt that the church should return to the stance of openness, so that those who wanted a place to pray would have one no matter what time of day. All the other churches in the community were locked, so if churches were to be opened, it would have to start with this one. How could the church reach out to the community from behind locked doors? The discussion in the vestry meeting was lengthy and sometimes heated. Those who wanted to maintain the status quo put forth arguments basically rooted in fear. In keeping with the status quo, the vestry voted to leave things the way they were—the front door would remain locked.

Personally, I feel that fear shows a lack of faith, and is a response to an evil spirit. You may not believe in evil spirits, or may object to the idea of evil spirits associated with the church, but Jesus encountered them often during his ministry and was able to send them away. The Lord's Prayer ends, "Rescue us from the evil one." If evil spirits are not real, why did Jesus tell us to pray to God to rescue us from them? It is my experience that when you ask God to remove an evil spirit that is causing you to fear, that spirit and the fear are gone—instantly. If you haven't experienced this phenomenon, I suggest that you try it the next time you sense that an evil spirit is present. I think that is the reason Jesus repeatedly cautions his disciples, "Oh you of little faith", when they exhibit fear. People with a strong faith, whom the Holy Spirit guides, are not afraid of change. The scriptural metaphor for this is "the wilderness". The group that was against opening the door was also very comfortable with the way things were and not inclined to go anywhere, least of all into unknown territory.

Although, at the time, it did not appear that anyone gave God credit for any part of the discussion, it is my opinion that God put the **idea** of unlocking the door and those arguments for it into the mind of someone in the parish. I have come to believe, and this story should confirm that during the course of normal and natural human affairs, God tries to communicate with people. I do not think that God has a voice, or uses language to communicate, but I feel very strongly, that He communicates through **ideas** that he somehow puts in our mind. In his book, "The critical Meaning of the Bible",[1] Raymond Brown asks, "'Does God speak?' And if one smilingly replies, 'Not in the physical sense of emitting sound waves,' there is still the question of whether God internally supplies words to the recipient of revelation and/or inspiration. I more than suspect

1 The critical Meaning of the Bible, Raymond E. Brown,S.S., Paulist Press, 1981

that there are theologians who as good scholastics would not blanch at saying that technically God does not think, has never had an idea, and makes no judgments, but would hesitate at saying that God does not speak."

Why would God want to start a discussion about a locked door at a church? Doors separate the inside from the outside or they separate rooms within a building; but when they are locked they can also separate people from each other. When the front door is locked what is inside is kept inside. What is inside a church is suppose to be the good news of God. Jesus asked his followers to take that good news to the world. The congregation of the parish was reluctant to do that. Also, when the front door is locked, what is outside stays outside; including elements of society that need to become familiar with that good news. Jesus' ministry appears to have been to the poor and oppressed; he made a point of ministering to the unclean and outcast people. Since you cannot minister to people from whom you are separated, I think God wanted the front door to be unlocked.

At the start of his ministry Jesus said, "The time has come. The kingdom of God is near. **Repent** and believe the good news." (Mark 1:15) The Greek word that is translated "repent" means, **"change direction"**. *Believing* means accepting an idea mentally, and then **putting that idea into action**. In other words, if you don't act on an idea you really don't believe it. Jesus did not qualify his statement by saying something like, "If you don't believe, repent" or "If you are a sinner, repent". He just said "Repent". He was including everyone, and what he taught was counter-cultural. He wanted them to **put into action** the things he was teaching and the things he was teaching were aimed at changing the world and that involved **changing the direction** of everyone's lives.

We have been taught to associate the word "repent" with sin—the connotation being, to stop sinning. I don't think that Jesus was talking to people who were doing things that were immoral. Most of what he teaches has nothing to do with morality. He was teaching how to become part of the Kingdom of God. I think he was suggesting a process of continuous change that would lead to a different kind of life, one he called eternal life in which we would no longer be separated from God. Jesus talked to anyone who would listen, so I think that he was speaking to all of us, wanting all of us to change, but not just change for the sake of change, but change to become servants to each other. He ministered in the open, not behind locked doors. He did not wait for those he was concerned about to come to him because he was concerned about everyone. He went out to them. Is this what we see in the actions of our society? Is this what the locked doors of our churches demonstrate? All these issues were involved in that locked door.

Even though there was resistance to change and a lack of communication with God, in this parish change was about to happen. In 1996 there was a break-in at the parish. The thieves gained entrance through an outside door, which was heavily damaged. They then gained entrance to the office, took some electronic equipment, and damaged this door as well. Within days the police caught the guilty parties and the stolen equipment was returned. In this instance the locked doors had not protected the property.

They had not done what it was hoped locking them would do.

No one saw God's hand in the break-in. I don't **know** whether God had anything to do with the break-in, but I **think** that he did. The stolen property was returned; no one was hurt; but the young men who broke in were poverty-stricken neighbors who could have used some direction in their lives.

I don't recall anyone being concerned with the thieves—an opportunity missed. The members of the congregation, if they were concerned at all, were all concentrating on how to prevent a reoccurrence; their thoughts were directed inward. The Psalmist repeatedly calls upon God's people to put their trust in the Lord.

Answer me when I call, O God of my right!
You gave me room when I was in distress.
Be gracious to me, and hear my prayer.

How long, you people, shall my honor suffer shame?
How long will you love vain words, and seek after lies?

But know that the Lord has set apart the faithful for himself,
The Lord hears when I call to him.

When you are disturbed, do not sin;
Ponder it on your beds, and be silent.

Offer right sacrifices,
And put your trust in the Lord.

There are many that say, "O that we might see some good!
Let the light of your face shine on us, O Lord"

You have put gladness in my heart
More than when their grain and wine abound.

I will both lie down and sleep in peace;
For you alone, O Lord, make me lie down in safety.
Psalm 4

How many people do you know that believe and follow the Psalmist's advice?

The evil spirit of fear was taking charge again and the spirit of fear always turns our thoughts inward. The parish had not learned that "Life **is not about me, it is about God**" to quote my spiritual director. When your attention is directed inward you don't see opportunities right in front of you. You also don't see God acting in the situation that you are concerned with. No one saw this as an opportunity to reach out and help these young men. The plight of the thieves was not the parish's concern at the moment. Those who violate the rules of society have to be punished, right? Well, as Christians, what do we do with this story?

The scribes and the Pharisees brought a woman who had been caught in adultery,

And placing her in the midst they said to him,

"Teacher, this woman has been caught in the act of adultery.

Now in the law Moses commanded us to stone such.

What do you say about her?"

This they said to test him that they might have

Some charge to bring against him

Jesus bent down and wrote with his finger on the ground.

And as they continued to ask him,

He stood up and said to them,

"Let him who is without sin among you

be the first to throw a stone at her."

And once more he bent down and wrote with his finger on the ground.

But when they heard it, they went away,

One by one beginning with the eldest, and Jesus was left alone

with the woman standing before him.

Jesus looked up and said to her,
"Woman, where are they? Has no one condemned you?"
She said, "No one, Lord."
And Jesus said, "Neither do I condemn you;
go, and do not sin again.
(John 8:3-7)

It seems to me that John is making several points with this story. Jesus accepts the accusation of the woman being an adulteress as fact but questions whether the accusers have a right to control her behavior. He lets the accusers condemn themselves by permitting anyone without sin to execute her according to God's law. No one can meet the criteria, so she is going to go unpunished. We believe that Jesus met the criteria, yet his only action was to tell her not to sin again. As was frequently his behavior, he did not follow the "law" as we understand it. He had no way to enforce that statement if she didn't obey it. Do we follow his teaching? And what does that tell you about some of the things we consider God's Law? Jesus, in this instance, let compassion overrule the law. Maybe he was trying to tell us that **compassion is the law**.

I suspect that God would have been happier with the parish if a few people had been concerned about the thieves. God may have been trying to awaken them to the conditions surrounding them in the community. God could have been using the break-in to change the lives of those who did the break-in, and he might have intended that this parish be the instruments of that change. After all, the parish members, like the members of all Christian churches, claim to be followers of Jesus. I believe that God was about to embark on a long and tedious road toward getting the parish members to understand what that means. All these possible opportunities were missed because the parish was looking inward to protect itself instead of looking outward to serve and looking to God for their security. I am convinced that God was trying to get the parish's attention, and eventually he did.

For a while no one related this incident to the locked doors, either, but finally, the incident did present the opportunity for God to inspire me to again bring up the subject of unlocking the front door. I don't remember any more why I was concerned that the front door to the church was locked, and that's one reason I think God gave me the idea. He could and did use me to make what he wanted happen even though I really didn't care about the front door being open. At any rate at the next meeting of the vestry I asked the question, "What is the value of a locked door?" The cost of repairing the two broken doors was a little over $300. Had the doors not been locked, it was my contention that there would have been no damage and the stolen items would still have been returned. The discussion was heated and lengthy. There was still the problem of safety, among other things. One question was, "Is God trying to tell us something?" You have probably heard that question posed many times in jest, but this time it was asked seriously. The discussion of that question had an effect on the decision. This time, by a close vote, 5 to 4, it was decided to unlock the front door. Those opposed to the decision had the vote recorded in the minutes of the vestry meeting by name. Never since has a roll call vote been recorded in the minutes of the vestry. Those opposed wanted to be sure that the rest of the congregation knew the names of those who agreed and disagreed.

As you can imagine, there was quite a bit of discussion about the decision. There were several parishioners who were angry and afraid and were opposed to the change. On the other hand, most of the members seemed to be willing to wait and see what would happen next. Churches are made up of people at different stages of the development of faith. When a community embarks on a change of direction, even though it is a small change, controversy usually develops if for no other reason than "we have never done it that way". It is helpful if there is a strong enough bond within the community to hold it together in spite of their differences. It also helps if people on both sides of the controversy are listening to those in opposition. In this case those opposed went along with the majority, but the different views on this decision remained a point of contention for quite a while.

At one point in the controversy someone suggested that unlocking the front door might increase the cost of the church's liability insurance, so it was decided to check with the insurance company. The insurance company's position was, and is, that the church, if it is to fulfill its purpose for being, is supposed to be open, so unlocking the door did not affect the insurance policy at all.

Although there were complaints and discussion for some time after the front door was unlocked, nothing really happened to alarm anyone, so the parish remained outwardly unified. Occasionally a stranger would come into the church to pray at night when no one was there. At the back of the church proper, just inside the door, there is a wooden stand with a guest book on it. Most of the time, the only way the parish knew that someone had come into the church was that they would sign the guest book and leave a comment, usually in the form of a thank you for the hospitality. These visits and comments helped to keep the front door open and strengthen the feeling that what they were doing was right and good.

Occasionally, there were overnight visitors and, when someone in the parish became aware of them, help was always forthcoming. Over the course of the next few years there were several opportunities to help individuals or families that came into the church as strangers. Some people in the congregation began to feel that maybe God was sending the strangers because he knew help would be available. I think that God was trying to make them aware that there were many more problems out there and there was much more work to be done. With time, the complaints and discussion ceased and the fact of the open front door was accepted as the "way it was" and most of the people felt good about what they were doing. I think that most of the members of the congregation had no idea of what this small change could lead to. A change had been made and not only did the parish survive the change, but it had opened the door for many more changes that were to come in the future. This small change in the policy of the parish was the beginning of a series of changes, all relating to that open door, which was to completely change the character of the parish.

It is very difficult to see what God is doing. Unless we have unusually strong faith we don't normally attribute what is going on around us to God's action. Only in retrospect, or from a distance in time, do we look back and see a pattern that we can attribute to God, as I am doing now. If we could learn to see God's action in the present we could accomplish more and have much less anxiety doing it. It seems to be a matter of faith. As you can tell, I believe that God acted to cause someone to bring up the discussion about the locked door in the first place, and I am convinced that heacted through me to finally get the door unlocked. You can decide for yourself.

Chapter 2
Food

Let me hear what God the Lord will speak,
For he will speak peace to his people,
To his faithful, to those who turn to him in their hearts
Psalm 85:8

Now that the front door of the church was open, God's next problem, if you want to put it that way, was either to get the congregation to reach out through that door, or to get those who needed help to go into the church. I say that it was God's problem because no one in the congregation was doing anything different to reach out. As it turned out, he seems to have chosen a little bit of both.

At this point in their history the parish had an adult Sunday school, which had only recently been started, but was growing. Shortly after the front door was unlocked, an adult study group was organized. Between the two groups, some of the congregation was being exposed to scripture in depth. This exposure was beginning to have an affect on their lives. I will have more to say about the importance of Christian Education in chapter 8, but I believe that because of their recent exposure to scripture they were more receptive to ideas for outreach. Some people in the study group got the **idea** that since the front door of the church was open all the time the parish had an opportunity to reach out to the community in the form of a small emergency food pantry that could be set up just inside the front door. I believe that the idea came from God. God was acting, again, in the life of the parish. I don't know whether they believed that or not, but it doesn't make any difference. They thought it was a good idea and it didn't matter to them where it came from. They acted on the idea.

At any given moment, there is a cacophony of ideas passing through our minds. When we are concentrating on some subject, these ideas are shoved into the background and we don't notice them. But if we let our mind wonder, we know that they are there. I used to wonder where these ideas came from because many of them didn't make sense to me. By studying these ideas, I have come to the conclusion that they have several sources, not all of them good. Most of them seem to come from our own ego because they are very "I" oriented. Some of them come from evil sources and they are not good for us or anyone else. Setting those aside for the moment, there are some that come from the Holy Spirit, and those we need to pay attention to. When we pay attention to those ideas we are what I term as "listening" to God. For me, most of the time in the past, those ideas were suggesting things that I didn't necessarily want to do. Often those ideas involved service to others that it was not convenient for me to do, so I ignored them. My recent experience has taught me that if we "listen", and act on what we "hear", we will be doing God's will and life can get very exciting.

Some people from the study group were "listening" and acted on the **idea.** The group called themselves "Act of Kindness". They put a small set of shelves inside the front door and stocked the shelves with a few basic items of food. There were usually several cans of vegetables, some breakfast cereal, a few cans of soup, and items like that. There would usually be six to ten different items on the shelves. A sign was placed above the set of shelves inviting anyone who was hungry to take what they needed, and then they waited to see what would happen. There was no publicity given to the fact that there was food inside the door just waiting to be taken by someone so it took quite a while before anything happened, but one day it was noticed that the food was gone. It was quickly replaced. The shelves started to become empty more often, but they were always refilled. The "Act of Kindness" group kept a close eye on the shelves and replaced the food whenever they noticed that the shelves were low on food or empty.

This idea gave new meaning to the open door policy and most of the congregation seemed to support the idea. Without the front door being open all the time, this type of ministry would not have been possible. This time there was no controversy associated with the change, in fact interest in the project grew. Not everyone in the congregation participated in keeping the shelves stocked so most of the congregation was not affected by the change, but even those not affected seemed to approve of the project. Other members of the congregation began paying attention to this little pantry and new people began joining the group that was keeping the shelves full. The activity level of the parish was noticeably raised.

God was acting on the congregation very slowly, but was making them aware of the poverty problem, especially the hunger problem in the community, in very small steps. The open door was getting members of the parish to reach out to some of the people in need. It was a small beginning that was destined to have a huge affect in the future.

When you reach out to other people, every once in a while something happens that warms the heart and makes you feel like you might be on the right track. The little emergency food pantry provided just such an occurrence. One evening a stranger came into the church. He had just gotten out of prison and had nowhere to stay. Somehow he found out the front door of the church was open, so he came inside and spent the night. The next morning he left very early to find a job. He had no success that day so he came back to the church a second night. As he approached the front door he saw a person leaving the church carrying a bag. When he came into the building he noticed that the food shelves were empty. The stranger happened to have some food stamps, so he went to a nearby grocery store and purchased food for the shelves with his food stamps. In the process of replacing the food he was discovered by a member of the parish who struck up a conversation with him, found out his predicament, and thanked him for being so generous. The visitor felt that the only way he could thank the church for its hospitality was to replace the food that had been taken. God certainly must have been at work in our visitor's life.

In most circumstances no one would give a thought to why the parish member
was at the church that evening. I have come to see God's hand in coincidences such as this so I no longer believe in coincidences. I think that God goes to a great amount of trouble to make things happen that look like coincidences. This is one way I can tell what God is doing in my life. I don't know the parish member's specific errand, but I strongly suspect that God wanted someone to be there to tell the rest of us what had happened so that we would be inspired. This incident made a lot of the congregation feel good about themselves and about what the parish was doing.

There came a point when the shelves would show up empty every day. This was a disturbing turn of events. The fact that it was disturbing illustrates how little the parish understood about the hunger problem and how far their attitude was from truly seeking a solution to the hunger problem. There was a lot of concern that maybe one person was taking all the food every day. The concern should have led the parish to make an effort to find out who was taking the food. If one person was taking it every day, that person was providing an opportunity for the parish to reach out to someone who was very much in need. There was no way that anyone could deduce from that experience the full extent of the problem that existed without getting more information. In a rural community, unlike a city, the problems of poverty are not as visible. In rural societies there is an invisible wall between the `haves' and the `have-nots'. This wall seems to be there by mutual consent, for the `have-nots' are not proud of their poverty and the `haves' for the most part don't want to be faced with the fact that the poverty is there. If they don't see it, they don't have to do anything about it. I don't mean to imply that various members of the parish were not aware that there were poor people in the community, or that many members of the parish were not already involved in outreach to the poor; it was just that, until now, they hadn't come face to face with the full extent of the problem. Now that their concern was more outwardly directed, they were being exposed to the problem in a new way and it was beginning to look worse than they had expected. Even when you are working on the fringes of the poverty problem you become aware of the immensity and complexity of the problem and for most of us this paralyzes us—where do you start if you really want to solve the problems of poverty? Most churches, if they do anything, start with a small project such as this, which only solves a small part of the problem, but it eases their consciences a little bit, and it is a start, but as long as it is just that one church, it goes no further than a start..

When the shelves were being emptied every day, some of the Act of Kindness Group began checking them more often, and refilling them. Some days they became empty twice. As you might expect, some of the parish became concerned that someone was abusing their generosity. It is my belief that when a program such as this begins to show success, evil sprits begin their work to try to destroy the program. In this case the attack was in the form fear of being taken advantage of. Maybe they were selling it, and using the money for drugs or alcohol or in some other way taking advantage of our generosity. I will have more to say about this problem in chapter 8. In reality, the amount of food on those shelves would probably not have met the needs of a family for even one day. The hunger problem in the community was much greater than any of us imagined. Had they been able to put a face on those taking the food, I am sure that some of the parish would have wanted to do more to alleviate the problem, but because those taking the food were able to remain anonymous, this didn't happen. When much later the parish did realize that the hunger problem was much greater than was generally known, it did do more toward solving the problem, but it took a while for that message to get across. What was important to me was the fact that this project was getting the attention of most of the parish and that there was concern for others who might have a hunger problem. What was discouraging was that their concern, at least at first, was that they someone was taking advantage of their generosity. Of course someone was taking advantage of their generosity. That is why the food was put there in the first place. Somehow, their concern had to be directed in a more positive direction and fortunately, it was. After much discussion it was decided that the real problem was that the project was beginning to get expensive. It was time to evaluate the program from the point of view of finding a solution to this new problem.

Projects like this should be evaluated periodically, and this was a good time to do the evaluating. If someone was taking all the food every day there was none left for anyone else who might need it. If there was one hungry person out there, there were probably more. At first, the question was, "How can we get whoever is taking the food to share?" Of course, if there were more, this small pantry was not going to solve the problem anyway, but no one was prepared at that time to suggest an alternate solution. They did decide to put a new sign next to the shelves asking a recipient to leave some for the next person. The sign did not change the situation; all the food kept disappearing.

It finally occurred to someone that there might be a family out there with no other means to get food except than this emergency pantry. There were also some indications that there was more than one person taking the food from the shelves. It didn't occur to anyone until later that God might be trying to make the parish aware that there was a hunger problem in the community that was not being addressed. Fortunately, no one wanted to stop putting the food out, so after much discussion and soul searching it was decided that the job of the parish was just to put the food on the shelves as long as they could afford the expense, and it was getting expensive. The parish decided it was up to God to get the food to the person in need. God had acted in this situation to change the attitude of those involved to an attitude of service. The parish was taking its first step toward serving the poor unconditionally. A little bit of God's message was coming through, but not enough to spur the parish into further action. God is both patient and persistent, and the parish was slowly learning.

Another very interesting and transforming incident occurred about that time and it also involved food. One Sunday the parish was having a congregational meeting, when a young couple came to the church. They had just moved to town, had spent all their money on an apartment, and were broke. They had a very young baby and they needed food and diapers. We interrupted the meeting and passed the hat, collecting exactly $75.00. For some reason, I was picked to take the couple to the supermarket and get them $75.00 worth of food and supplies. At the supermarket I told them to just go though the store and get what they needed. For some reason, it never occurred to me that there should be some control on how much they decided to get. That is, it didn't occur to me until they came to the checkout counter. What would I do if they picked out more than the $75.00 worth of merchandise? I think that the evil spirits were at work on me, again. After about 20 minutes the couple came to the checkout counter with a shopping cart full of groceries and diapers. I needn't have worried. I don't know how God arranges these things, but when they went through the checkout counter the bill came to $75.10 and I did happen to have a dime. I took the family and the food back to their apartment. When I got back to the church the congregational meeting was still in progress, so I told them the story. I may be wrong, but I think God got everyone's attention at that meeting. That was probably the most effective Sunday school lesson we had ever had. It was also the largest audience that the Sunday school had ever had—could it have been by God's arrangement? Everyone left the meeting feeling very good about the things that the parish was doing. Also this was the first incident where everyone involved knew that God had acted in the life of the parish and the effect was small, but it was in the right direction.

Churches are meant to be communities that reach out to people both within and outside. Not only did "Acts of kindness" help people outside the parish who needed help, it raised the interest of more of the members inside the parish. They felt good about the fact that the parish was helping people in the community and more people wanted to become involved, even if only slightly. This project seemed to overcome some of the inertia that existed in the group that didn't want to change. That very simple, small outreach project was strengthening the parish and changing its outlook.. God was making progress; however, for the next several years no new projects were started.

There were problems developing in both the diocese and the national church that caused the attention of the parish to again be directed inward. Controversies surfaced that were far more serious than the unlocking of the front door and the parish suffered some severe setbacks in both size and income. There was a change in priests, so for a while the parish was in a state of adjustment. For over a year supply priests conducted the services and the planning and operation of the parish was done completely by the laity. There was no priest to take care of all the routine things that have to be done to keep a parish going. The laity had to take ownership of the parish, so more people got active. The financial status of the parish also improved markedly, because the expenses were much less without a priest. In retrospect, I now think that God was strengthening the laity in the parish, getting more of the active members to appreciate the value of the parish in their everyday lives. When the time was right, God sent another priest to the parish. That is another story, but this time there were several members of the parish that felt very strongly that God had sent the new priest. Whether it was because of the controversies, or because the parish was realizing their need for a priest or maybe some other reason, the parish had turned to God in at least this small way, and recognized that God had responded to their need. God was becoming more relevant in the life of the parish.

Chapter 3
A Transforming Call

Then the Lord said, "I have seen the affliction of my people
Who are in Egypt, and have heard their cry because of their
Taskmasters; I know their sufferings and I have come down
to
Deliver them out of the hand of the Egyptians, and to bring
them
Up out of that land to a good and broad land,
A land flowing with milk and honey.——-
And now, behold, the cry of the people of Israel has come
to me,
and I have seen the oppression with which the Egyptians
oppress them.
Come, I will send you to Pharaoh that you may bring forth
my people,
the sons of Israel, out of Egypt."
But Moses said to God, "Who am I that I should go to
Pharaoh,
And bring the sons of Israel out of Egypt?"
He said, "But I will be with you;"
Exodus 3:7-12 (Revised Standard Version)

I am convinced that there are spiritual forces in this world
that we do not understand. I don't know how they work or

how we can interact with them, but I am convinced that they exist. Until the age of enlightenment, when it became possible and then necessary to explain all phenomena with technology, the common world view believed in and recognized that these spiritual forces existed and were active in the lives of human beings. But since technology has not as yet found a way to measure these forces, belief in them has passed out of the common worldview. The common worldview is that all things that are real are made up of matter and energy, and follow known rules of behavior. That worldview puts spiritual forces in the realm of superstition or the supernatural. We can't define or measure these spiritual forces, but we can experience them and once you have experienced them you know that they are real.

As I said in Chapter 1, I feel that God has been communicating with me. I say communicating because I am not hearing voices, or seeing visions, or dreaming dreams, but many of the thoughts that pass through my mind are not of my doing. It is my practice to sit quietly for 15 minutes or so before I go to bed and study whatever thoughts go through my mind. Often I get insights into solutions to situations that I am involved in. It is a wonderful experience and helpful. I would like to think that God has been trying to help me in this way, but could never be sure.

Scripture has many examples of God communicating with mankind. In Genesis 6:13-21 God "spoke" to Noah. In Genesis 12:1-3 God "spoke" to Abram. In Genesis 15 God communicates with Abram in a vision. In the third chapter of Exodus, God "spoke" to Moses from a burning bush. There are many other examples of God communicating with mankind in the scriptures, but in this day and age does anyone really believe that God still communicates with mankind or ever did for that matter? Does our view of reality discount the experiences of the sages of antiquity who wrote these ancient stories? I very much wanted to believe that it was God who was giving me all these ideas, but I have been educated in the sciences, so without some other evidence of the existence of spirits; I didn't feel secure in basing my life on the idea that God was giving me advice.

I didn't until one Sunday morning in February of 2003 when I awoke knowing that during the night, or possibly just before I awoke, God had "spoken" to me. I don't know how I knew this, but it was as clear as the sky that morning. I don't remember dreaming…I don't remember hearing a voice. Nevertheless, I knew that I had been given the job of creating a homeless shelter in the town of the parish. It was a lot like hearing a voice. The message was clear, but it didn't come through my ears, so, technically, it would not be correct to say God spoke to me but in the biblical sense, he did. I will just say that God communicated with me, and I got the message. My first thought was, "What just happened here? Is my mind playing tricks on me?" I sat on the edge of the bed and thought for a while. The more I thought about it, the fewer details I could remember. It wasn't frightening and it wasn't the first time God had *communicated* with me, but it was definitely clearer to me than I had ever experienced before. It wasn't a suggestion or advice either—it was an order, a lot like God gave to Moses. There was no need for a discernment process. I felt that I had no choice but to do the job God had given me to do, but I had no idea how to do it or where to start. I also knew right away that my life had been changed completely.

As I have previously stated, I have never had any interest in poverty issues of any kind. In fact, I was one of those church members who got upset at the church leaders when pressure was put on the membership to get involved with the social issues of our time. So this was not some hidden ambition that I suddenly decided to try. As a matter of fact, I didn't even know whether or not there was a homeless problem in the town.

Since this event I have several times reviewed that third chapter of Exodus and have found similarities between my experience and that of Moses. Although Moses had the background and training to do the job that God wanted done, setting the Hebrew people free from the power of Pharaoh in Egypt was not a thought that had been foremost in Moses' mind. Scripture doesn't say how Moses knew he was in the presence of the Sacred, but he knew. Moses had the background and training to do the job. My background and training was such that I had the tools to do the job, also, but I had never thought of doing anything like that. Moses gave God several reasons why he wasn't the man for the job, but he knew that in the end he was going to have to do what God wanted. So did I. I knew that I had had a `burning bush' experience. A `burning bush' experience is literally a life changing experience. It is almost as if time stops and God puts a whole new value system in your brain. There are other examples of this type of experience in scripture, such as Saul's encounter on the road to Damascus. When you come face to face with the sacred, your life changes immediately. You still make the decisions, but they are based on a whole new set of data. My question was then, and still is, how did I know that my orders came from God? How do I or did I know that I had come face to face with the sacred? Moses had the same problem and God showed him some tricks that convinced Moses. What finally convinced me was something that came later when I started the project.

Since that February morning my life and my worldview has been transformed. When I said "yes" to God's request, my whole outlook on life changed. Now I can understand how Paul's worldview was completely turned around by his experience on the road to Damascus. It seemed like my reason for being alive changed, and the change was definitely a blessing. I went to church services that morning, as I always did on Sunday morning, but this morning my mind was preoccupied with my waking experience and looking for some explanation of what I had sensed. What I had experienced is not something that you can talk about in casual conversation without the person you are talking to thinking that you have lost your mind. I had one clue about how to start the project. I live in a town 35 miles from the town in which the parish is located. Since I was supposed to start the shelter in the town where I attend church, the project was probably supposed to be church-connected.

In the parish I am on the evangelism committee and that committee had a meeting scheduled after the service. The discussion at that meeting was about how the parish could become better known in the community. The conversation eventually came around to talking about outreach projects that we could do that might get us exposure to the general public. I recognized that this might be the way I was supposed to start the project so I suggested that we start a homeless shelter. The idea was not greeted with enthusiasm, in fact, as I recall, no one said anything. The suggestion was completely ignored and the discussion continued around other ideas. My immediate thought was that this must not be the way God wanted the project done. My mind was searching for clues and it wasn't finding any. No decision was reached at that meeting but it was decided that each of us should give some thought to what we could do and bring those thoughts up at a meeting the following month. If God was "talking" to anyone on the committee they sure weren't listening

At the next meeting, no one had any suggestions that brought any enthusiasm from the others on the committee. With some hesitation, I again suggested that we start a homeless shelter. Maybe this was to be the vehicle by which the shelter would come about. This time I got several responses, all of which amounted to the project being much too big for our little congregation. Although I didn't realize it at the time, this was a clue for how I was to proceed with the project. Again the suggestion was turned down, and again no decision was made on what we could do. I don't know why I wasn't upset by my suggestion being turned down, but I wasn't. Even though I knew what I intended to do, I still had no idea how to get the project started. But I felt very strongly that when the time was right the necessary help would turn up. Looking back on it from my present perspective, I think God was telling me to be patient. It wasn't time, yet. Maybe those who were to help me do God's job were not ready yet.

Before my February epiphany I probably would have been upset by the group rejecting my idea, but I was at peace with the situation. I didn't know how God wanted me to proceed, and I figured that there was going to be a different way presented to me, so I should be patient. After the meeting the comments about the project being too big for our little parish kept running around in my mind. Maybe we should get other churches involved in the project. God was again communicating with me.

Again, the following month the committee met. There were still no other suggestions from members of the committee, so I repeated my suggestion that we start a homeless shelter. The project might be too big for the parish to do alone, but it wasn't too big for the entire Christian community to take on. I pointed out that scripture repeatedly calls for God's people to take care of the poor and oppressed. Although many churches don't believe it, God's people includes more than just one parish. My comments started a discussion that resulted in one woman on the committee, who in the past had been involved with starting other community projects, volunteering to help me get started. After more discussion the committee warmed to the project and decided we should give it a try.

I believe that by the third month, God had all his ducks in a row and the things necessary for this project to be successful were now just waiting for someone to find them and use them. No one person, nor one church, has either the resources or the personnel to accomplish a project as large and complex as a homeless shelter, especially if it is a shelter in which the emphasis is on changing the way the clients look at life. But the *idea* was given to me that the 'Body of Christ', acting in a unified manner, could accomplish the task and would benefit from the experience.

Paul, in many of his letters, encourages his fledgling churches to become unified and function as the 'Body of Christ'. The same principle applies today, even more so than in the first century. My question was, "How do we get the different denominations to act in a unified manner on the project?" The various denominations each go their separate ways. They would rather compete with each other than work together. In many cases several churches will have the same outreach projects, yet carry them out separately rather than combine and have a greater impact on the problem. They differ on topics such as who is 'saved' or whether the Bible has to be taken word for word or can be interpreted, or who is acceptable in the church and such inconsequential things as that, while their neighbors go hungry and are homeless. They literally "strain out gnats and swallow camels", making token efforts with the poor. The question of how would we get them to work together is an example of how we miss opportunities by feeling that we have to do everything, overlooking God's efforts on the project. God was already at work on this problem and it would turn out to be a non-issue.

The first question my partner asked me was, "Are you sure that we have a homeless problem in the community?" I had to admit that I had no idea whether or not we had a problem, but I felt confident that we did and I told her about my February morning experience. Why would God tell me to start a homeless shelter if there was no need for one? One answer to that question could have been, "You are the one who thinks God told you to start a homeless shelter, not me." I suspect that something like that was going through her mind at the time. Anyway, we decided to check with some of the social service agencies in the county to see if they had any data on the extent of the homeless problem.

The State of Ohio handles issues of employment and welfare through a large agency in each county called Job and Family Services. We decided to start there, so my partner called for an appointment. She called on a Tuesday morning and got an appointment for the next day. We met with the director of the agency and her second in command on Wednesday morning. The director started the meeting with this statement. "This is a strange circumstance. On Monday we had our annual planning meeting and the main topic for discussion was `What are we going to do about the homeless problem in the county?' On Tuesday morning you called and asked for a meeting to discuss the homeless problem in the county." I am totally serious when I say that God was waiting for that meeting to occur before he gave me a partner with which to start the project. With the Director's statement I knew two things: 1. We had a homeless problem in the county that someone needed to do something about; and 2. This was the proof that God was giving me that he was real and had really visited me. God definitely had given me that order and he was in charge of this project. I wasn't surprised by the need, but I was very much encouraged. I knew from that point on that we would eventually have a shelter, and that I wasn't going crazy thinking that I had been commissioned by God to get this job done.

As far as I was concerned, the meeting could have ended right there. We had the information we had come for. We did, however get more information during the meeting. We found out that the people at that agency knew that there was a problem; and that it was a large problem. But they kept no records on individual cases of homelessness, so no statistics were available. They didn't have the data we thought we would need to sell the issue to the other churches. They just shipped the homeless persons to the neighboring cities where there were shelters (there were only 2 shelters within 50 miles of the county). Out of sight, out of mind.

In talking with other agencies, we found the same thing. They all knew that there was a problem, but they kept no records, nor did any of them try to do anything to alleviate the problem. That attitude, unless changed, would guarantee that the community would always have a homeless problem. My guess is that attitude is common to most communities and that is one reason the homeless problem exists. It is easy to be critical of situations such as this, especially when you know very little about the system. In the years since that first meeting I have learned a lot about poverty, hunger and homelessness, so I am less critical of the people involved in relief efforts, but I am very skeptical of the overall attempts that society has made to solve the problems. Of course, I am including myself in that last statement, because until this point, I had never been in favor of social action programs myself. Maybe that former point of view had something to do with God tapping me to fix this problem.

At least one "cause for concern" can be leveled at all the social service agencies in this county, and that is that there is very limited communications between the agencies. When one of their clients has a problem that involves more than one agency, which is true in most cases, there is no mechanism whereby the agencies can work together, or at least keep each other informed of the problems outside their area of responsibility. Unless there is a system or mechanism that can foresee someone using the data, what is the good of keeping records of problems that fall outside an agency's area of responsibility. Until we develop a system that attacks the poverty problem as a whole, we will have limited success in reducing poverty.

After surveying several social service agencies, and satisfying ourselves that there was, indeed, a serious problem in the county, we decided to elicit the support of several of the large churches in the two biggest communities in the county. We took an assertive approach:. "We are going to have a homeless shelter in this county. We feel that the homeless problem is an issue of justice, and that God wants his church to become an agent for justice. Therefore we would like your church to join us on a committee to make this happen. We would like you to recruit someone from your congregation to join our committee who is interested in solving the problem of homelessness. We do not want the pastor—he has enough work to do. We want a few dedicated people." We needed people who were willing to make sacrifices and do whatever was necessary. And they responded. God was working ahead of us.

We ended up with twelve laypersons (and three pastors who were interested enough in the problem that they wanted to be a part of the committee even though they hadn't been recruited) from eleven congregations representing nine denominations. At our first meeting, held in July of 2003, we also had representatives from three of the social service agencies and the mayor of one of the towns. A little bit about the makeup of the committee is appropriate at this point. Four of the men and one woman were retired. Three of those four men had been business executives. One woman was a semi-retired teacher who was still involved with adult education, and another was a teacher who was still teaching in the county system. One man was a lawyer; another was a human resources director with a corporation. One woman was the wife of a doctor, had three school-aged children at home and was in charge of the social outreach budget for her church. Two other women were still working full time. All these people were very active leaders in their respective churches. These same people stayed with the project until after the shelter was a reality and they all worked hard to see it blossom.

We knew from the very beginning that none of us had any idea as to where to start or how to proceed. None of us had any knowledge or experience of the hoeless problem. That turned out to be a blessing because we all started out to explore the problem from as many aspects as we could think of. This took a lot of time, and delayed the project becoming a reality for at least a year, but when we finally put the project together we knew what we wanted the shelter to look like and what needed to be accomplished.

The first thing the committee wanted to assure themselves of again was that there truly was a homeless problem in our communities. The committee again talked to various social service agencies and got the same answers my partner and I had gotten. We then researched demographic records, and again found nothing conclusive. Finally one of the committee took the time to survey ninety churches in the county to find out how often they came in contact with homeless people. That survey found enough instances of homelessness that the committee became convinced that there was a problem although we still had no quantitative answer.

We invited landlords to one of our meetings to get their view of the housing problem in regards to renters and rental prices. We invited realtors to another meeting to talk about property that might be available for a shelter and the public relations problems that we were likely to encounter when we picked a spot for the shelter. We invited Salvation Army leaders who had experience in running shelters to another meeting to discuss the real conditions that occur with running a shelter. We had several committees visit facilities around the state to get some knowledge of how to proceed as well as what services we should provide.

By July of 2004 we knew what we wanted our shelter to look like and the services we wanted it to provide. Convinced that a shelter was necessary, we were ready to move ahead. We had developed a mission statement, so we were ready to proceed. I feel that it is very important with a complex project like this that a mission statement be developed as a first step as a means of keeping everyone focused on what they are trying to accomplish. It helps to keep the group from being side-tracked. Our next step was to incorporate. The lawyer on our committee volunteered to take care of this responsibility and he did. We had picked a shelter that we had visited several times as a model. We decided it was time to make public the fact that we were going to have a shelter in the county. The various local news media had gotten wind of the project and had several times asked to be let in on what we were doing. We did not want any pro and con discussion going on in the community until we knew what we were going to do. We had been putting the news media off because we had encountered very negative attitudes toward the project during our learning phase. Now we knew what the problem was and how we were planning to proceed, so we told them what we were planning. We had no money, no budget, no location, but we knew what we were going to do and how we were going to proceed. At that point, I think that most of the committee felt reasonably confident that we were going to be successful. That confidence would be severely tested as we moved into the hard work of the project.

We had encountered skepticism with everyone we had talked to. Two of the three clergypersons on the committee were very skeptical about our ability to raise enough money. Churches are always short of the money they need to do the things they'd like to do. Even they had overlooked God's part in the project. We didn't raise the money, God did. We had decided to get started with private money because we didn't want the red tape and interference that we thought came with government financing. We had to be sure that we had enough public support to keep the shelter operating. This was a very good decision and played an important part in our success for several reasons. First it made it necessary for us to build a very strong case and a viable program to convince the public that we knew what we were doing. This was critical for financial support. Later, we found out that because we had the public behind us, we were able to secure a lot of government support that we would not have had otherwise. Neither the government nor most foundations will give financial support for startup money. Both will support prjects like this once they are up and running. The problem with government funding is that it is easy to get spoiled by it and stop campaigning for private funding. It seems we all would still like to have the government take care of the problem. Also, we decided to have at least six months of operating expenses in the bank before we opened our doors. It is important to note that we maintained that cushion for quite a while, and the reserve funds inspired public confidence that we were going to be around for the long haul. Such confidence inevitably generates more support. We were concerned about the public reaction to a homeless shelter because of the image the public has about homeless people. We were told over and over again that when we picked a location we would have a lot of controversy and criticism…that we would face the attitude. "Not in my neighborhood". There was even some concern that the public would not support it financially.

Next we had to come to agreement on the rules under which we could accomplish our goals and also keep everyone safe. During our conversations it became obvious that we had the same image of a homeless person that the general public had. This image turned out to be only partly correct, but we realized that we needed someone on the committee that had experience with the homeless. God again stepped in—he was way ahead of us. When we incorporated, the committee became the Board of Trustees for the Corporation. One of the pastors, the senior pastor of his denomination in the county, announced that he could not be on the board because he was already over-committed, but that there was a new pastor at another local church in his denomination who would take his place on the committee. This new pastor and her husband had been volunteer managers of an emergency shelter in another community for the past seven years. She became amember of the board, and eventually, he became the director of the shelter. It is my firm belief that they were sent by God to this community so that he could run the shelter. God will and does provide if you let him and are doing what God wants done.

While the board was working on the rules, the various church organizations began raising money for the new shelter. Shortly after we were incorporated, the parish gave the new organization seed money of $500.00 to cover the administrative type expenses that we were now bound to incur. The Roman Catholic grade school in one of the communities held a fund-raiser, done mostly by the kids, and raised over $3000.00 to help us get started. That Christmas, one of the churches involved in the project decided to test the waters of public sentiment. It was their practice to take a special offering at their Christmas Eve services and divide the money between a local charity and an international project. They decided to give our committee the local half and told us that normally they collect about $2500.00. The pastor was concerned that the idea of a homeless shelter would reduce the amount collected. He needn't have been concerned. God does provide. Their collection was over $7500.00—three times their normal offering. This was a great confidence booster for the board, who by this time felt that we were looking at an annual budget for the shelter of about $150,000. It also showed us again that God was working like an advanced agent. He was out in front of us clearing the way.

It took several meetings and much discussion, to settle on the rules under which the shelter would operate. The project would have been at a standstill without the expertise of our newest members, who had major input in formulating the rules and restrictions. The board decided:

We would serve single adults, both men and women, and families, all in the same structure.

- The shelter would need a staff of a director, two part-time case workers and a security firm to supplement the director
- The case workers' jobs would be to work out a plan with each client as they came to the shelter that, if followed

46

would get them back on their feet economically and back into normal housing of some type.

- People could stay in the shelter for up to 3 months provided the client followed the plan that had been made, became employed and stayed employed while they were in the shelter.
- No smoking inside the facility
- Drug or alcohol use would be reason for removal from the shelter,
- Everyone who came to the shelter would be subjected to a background check
- Once in the shelter they had to be there every night by 10 PM.
- The residents would be required to use the services of whatever social service agencies could help them in their particular case.
- The security firm was included in the plan so that supervision would be on hand at all times. All this was done before any campaign for funds was begun and before the search for a building to house the shelter was started.

When all the planning was complete and everyone was agreed on what was to be accomplished, the board started concentrating on raising the money and finding the facility and the people to make it a reality. In planning a project this size it is necessary, in my opinion, that all these basic decisions are settled before trying to put in place the capital equipment necessary to make it a reality. It is because we did it that way that the shelter has been a resounding success from the day it opened its doors, and it has been able to help many, many individuals and families get back on their feet. I would advise any group that wants to start a large and complicated project like this to proceed in this fashion. The details of finances and facilities can wait until all the planning is complete.

We had now reached the spring of 2005. As the Board was planning its financial campaign to raise the $150,000 budget, out of the blue, came two $25,000.00 contributions from people who didn't even live in the state, but had connections to the county and wanted to support our efforts. More providing on God's part. I have become aware of the details behind one of those contributions and am convinced, as was the donor, that God had his hand in it. The donor had made an unexpoected profit on a business deal, and had the feeling that he was supposed to give it to our project, which he knew about.

The Board of Trustees now had nearly $60,000.00 in the bank, and the organization was qualified as a tax-deductible charitable organization. It was time to start raising money. We studied the possibility of sending letters to everyone in the two zip codes that defined the two largest communities in the county. We found that the cheapest that we could get that accomplished would be a little over $5000.00, and we were reluctant to spend that much of our limited resources on the gamble that a letter would raise more than that amount. Then someone in the community who knew of the project and was very much in favor of what we were doing found out about our dilemma and made the decision for us by footing the bill. Another case of God providing. The letter got a response of over $10,000.00 immediately and served as a public announcement that we were committed to having a shelter. Again, God was providing, and the response was very encouraging to the Board. We now had 50% of our annual operating budget. We had the money to open the shelter but we still had no shelter or any staff.

The site committee had looked at houses and buildings and more houses and buildings, with no success. The big stumbling block was the money to buy and repair a suitable structure. We did not want to commit any of our operating money to obtaining a building. There were buildings available, but the committee found that we were looking at around $250,000 to buy a facility and renovate it so that it would be suitable for a shelter. The committee was very discouraged and was about ready to give up when a member of the committee discovered that his church owned a building that was to be torn down; but they didn't have the money to demolish it. This church had another dilemma—it was costing them over $10000 a year for maintenance even though they weren't using it. The building was a three-story apartment house that was essentially standing empty. He suggested to the church's board of trustees that they lease it to us until such time as they had the money to demolish the building.

The church's first thought was that it would cost the shelter a lot of money to bring the building up to code. We suggested that they allow us to have the building inspectors, who regulate such things, inspect the building and tell us what we would have to do to use it. They gave us permission, and the inspectors came. When they were finished we had a very short list of things that the fire department wanted changed, but essentially, since the building was originally built as an apartment building, the grandfather clauses applied, and it was not subject to the current building codes. (God was still with us.) The changes that we needed to make cost us about $10,000 and were paid for by more grants from local foundations.

After some negotiations, the church leased the building to the shelter company for $1.00 per year on a two-year renewable lease. God had again provided, this time in a very large way. Since the building was going to be demolished, they gave us permission to remodel it as we pleased. During the summer of

2005 this was the center for volunteer activity for the whole Christian community in the county.

The inside was repainted

A few new partitions were put up to properly separate the sections that would be for single men from the single women and from the family area.

The old kitchens, (there were six of them in the building,) were removed

and one new small one was built by the students at the vocational high school.

The bathrooms were redone and new fixtures installed.

The fire escape was repaired and repainted.

All the windows were washed

a lot of electrical work was done

new water heaters were installed.

All this work was done at no cost to the shelter. Where money had to be spent,

the bills were paid by one of the several local foundations. By the way, we never did hear the complaint of, "not in my neighborhood". There is a private home next to the shelter. Before we opened, I called on the residents of that home to tell them of our plans and to get their reaction. Their reaction was positive. They thought it was a good idea.

By the end of August we had everything we needed to begin operations. The only thing that was left to be done was to hire and train a staff. We advertised for a director, and after several interviews, decided that we hadn't found the person we felt could handle the job. At this point, the pastor, who had helped manage the shelter where they had lived before, suggested to me that her husband might be persuaded to take the job, at least at the beginning. With that information, I had a long talk with him. He was in business for himself and his business wasn't local, but it was a high-tech business that he felt he could keep going part time. He decided to take the challenge. We hired him and let him select his staff of two part-time caseworkers.

One of those caseworkers has an interesting story. She and her husband, the pastor of a local church, had come to the community early in the summer. They had moved from Florida, where she was finishing her degree work as a social worker, with emphasis on counseling. She only wanted part-time work and we wanted what she had. Was she sent? I think so and so does she, but that's only our opinion. She was hired, has since become a licensed counselor, is now full time, and has helped dozens of people get back on their feet. We had our staff and were ready to go. We had everything we needed and had done all our homework.

Then we experienced an unexpected problem. The Board was reluctant to take that final step, beyond which there was no turning back. They came up with dozens of little things that they wanted settled or done before the shelter was opened.

September passed, and still no decision was made to open. I now think that there were other preparations that God was making, so he wasn't ready for us to open. Finally a few members convinced the rest of the Board to hold an open house early in October, knowing that when that had been accomplished, we would have to open. On October 31, 2005, the shelter opened its doors. Twelve days later, the shelter was full to capacity, which we had established at 20 people. (So much for the consensus in the community that there were no homeless people in the county.) We had room to expand and we knew that we had to do it immediately, since winter was upon us. By the end of January 2006 we had expanded to accommodate 35 residents, the legal capacity of the building. Since that time we have operated between 25 clients and full capacity all the time. Most of the time the shelter has been full with a waiting list.

So what did we learn during this exercise? I think most of the Board realizes that we are just stewards of God's shelter. Every time that we hit a roadblock, when we had just about exhausted our ideas of how to get past the problem, something happened to make it disappear. Even the slow learner could eventually see that some other force was at work here and that the unseen, undefined force was God. Every time we had a seemingly insurmountable problem, it was solved by circumstances that none of us had anything to do with. You would think that the Board would continue to be aware of the direction that God wants this project to go, but being human beings, we still fall back into the habit of thinking that we have to come up with the solutions. As a result, sometimes the problems persist for a long time until someone is inspired enough to listen to God. When that happens, everything is taken care of. Eventually, God gets through to one of us to make the changes necessary to keep the project going.

We now know that there are a lot of homeless in the community that won't come to the shelter, and we know that that number has always been large. Why were there no statistics available when we started the project? In a rural county such as ours it is still socially unacceptable to be poor. If we were willing to seriously study the root causes of homelessness and hunger, I'm sure that we would find real solutions. As it is we want to solve the problems by criticizing the way things are and asking the government to give us more money. I can say that for sure the root cause of poverty in general is not economic. The root causes reside in our psychological make-up, in our approach to education, in our approach to mental health and in our spirituality just to name a few. None of these have anything to do with economics.

From the day the shelter opened the community has been behind it. The shelter has served to tear down that invisible wall between the `haves' and the `have-nots' in the county. The community as a whole has seen the homeless problem and they have responded in amazing ways. Daily, the shelter receives donations of things we didn't even know that we needed. We find ways to put them to use in alleviating some part of the poverty problem. The shelter has become a center for the community to minister to the poor and the need for many more projects has become apparent. Many people have come forward wanting to help. In our community enough people are looking honestly at the causes, that we are slowly correcting some of these problems ourselves. The government is helping a little with money, but the new programs that will be necessary can and will be developed locally. More churches and more people are getting involved with solving other social problems in the community and this is the only way those problems will be solved. One on one involvement on a local level is the key to success. We know, for instance, that the shelter is only about half the size it needs to be to meet the needs of the homeless in the community who are willing to come to a shelter. We also know that we need other shelters with different rules, aimed to help the homeless who can't or won't come into our shelter. There is a need for rehabilitation facilities of various types to help those who are mired in various addictions.

As people leave the shelter and become contributing members of the community, the image of the homeless person is gradually changing in the community. Most encouraging of all, some of the alumni of the program are coming back as volunteers to help those still involved in the program to solve their problems and change their lives.

Chapter 4

Jesus answered them, "Truly I tell you,
Not only will you do what has been done to the fig tree,
But even if you say to this mountain, `Be lifted up
And thrown into the sea,' it will be done.
What ever you ask for in prayer with faith, you will receive."
Matthew 21:21,22

Community reaction

The shelter does not just put a roof over the head of persons who have no place to sleep. It is more like a halfway house than an emergency shelter. It was designed to help the unemployed find work, the mentally ill get connected with mental health facilities and addicts get connected with rehabilitation workers. In short, it is there to help people get back on their feet. The caseworkers help connect the homeless to whatever social service agency is needed. It is also a place where a person gets a chance to change his/her life for the better, and the residents are encouraged to do so The staff arranges for classes to be held in the evening to teach the residents how to budget, how to interview for a job, how to shop economically, and other skills useful in caring for a house or apartment. They also try to convince the guests that they need to take charge of their lives and that no one else can solve their problems for them. They must do it themselves.

Dinner is supplied every evening by one of the churches or other community organizations. If the homeless person needs clothing the shelter staff connects them with one of several clothing pantries in the community. Once in the shelter the resident can stay for 90 days provided he/she follows the rules. If they make the attempt this is more than enough time for most people to get back on their feet. What we didn't realize when we planned the shelter was that most of the homeless are not ready to make the attempt. Even most people at the bottom of the economic ladder are unwilling to change.

Once the shelter was open and people could see that there was a great need, the community responded. Organizations throughout the community got actively involved in trying to meet the needs of the guests. I believe that God was speaking to a lot of people in the community. They brought clothing, food, cleaning supplies, toilet articles, bedding, furniture, appliances, and money into the shelter on a daily basis. (The furniture and appliances are given to the residents who have none when they move into an apartment or a house.) The magnitude of this response was completely unexpected, but it shouldn't have been. By this time we should all have realized that when you are doing God's work, **God will provide.** With all the miracles that we had experienced during the organizing and establishing of the shelter, you would have thought that we would have learned that God would give us what we needed to make **His** shelter a success.

Volunteers

Another important way that the community's compassion was expressed was the ease with which the shelter staff was able to recruit volunteers to help. Volunteers are an integral part of the operation of the shelter. When the shelter is fully staffed, there are two volunteer receptionists seated just inside the door from 9 AM until 8 PM. Greeting new arrivals and answering the telephone are two of many tasks they perform. They record all the events that take place at this desk, such as receiving donations; greeting visitors and connecting them with the guest(s) they are visiting. They take messages for the guests and pass them on, log the guests in and out so that the staff can keep track of their activities, and perform many more routine tasks. But the most important job that they do is to get to know the guests, have conversation with them, and become roll models for them. By their very presence they let the resident know that there are people in the community who really care about them and care what happens to them. Since the residents are usually lonely, this is very important for getting them in a positive frame of mind when they go out looking for employment. Much of the success that the shelter has in getting people back on their feet is due to these resident/ volunteer relationships. The volunteer can't make the necessary changes for them but he/she can go a long way toward bringing them out of their depression just by listening to them. When the homeless person begins to feel that someone else cares, his/her self-image improves and sometimes he/she is ready to change.

In a community project like this—and the homeless shelter has become a community project—volunteering to give time and effort to the project is very important. I have become convinced that poverty problems will only be solved when communities respond to the problems through volunteerism because only through volunteerism can the type of relationships be developed that will bring about the needed change. Many of the volunteers at the shelter work there several times a week, taking regular shifts every week. They get to know the people who have been in the shelter for a while and spend a lot of time trying to encourage and befriend them. There is an excitement among the volunteers that is contagious. At first most of the volunteers came from the churches involved in the project, but after a while they began coming from other parts of the community, too. Volunteering to help other people has its very significant rewards. As Jesus told the crowd and his disciples, "The greatest among you will be your servant." (Matthew 23:11).

What are the Homeless Like?

As I mentioned earlier, the shelter was the first close exposure to the homeless culture for most of the Board of Trustees as well as for the volunteers. We had assumed that most of the guests who came would be motivated by their conditions to look for a job and be ready to get their lives together. In the case of the majority of homeless people, this is a bad assumption. I put the homeless in five categories; the vagabond; those who have lost their job; the addict; those with mental issues; and the helpless.

The vagabond is the panhandler or free spirit who wants the freedom involved in his/her life style. This type usually won't come into a shelter like this one, or if they do it is for a very brief stay, then they move on. This type of homeless person will always be with us. This is also the stereotype that the general public puts all homeless people in. The other four categories of homeless will come to the shelter, but each must be handled differently for the shelter to be successful in helping them.

The second category, the person who is unaccustomed to being out of work, homeless, and broke, who lost his/her job, has been unable to find another, and usually has debts that have finally caught up with them is usually in the shelter only long enough to get over the shock of being homeless, find another job, get the debts under control and save enough money to get a place to live. Depending on their debt load, this may only take a few weeks. This type of homeless person is usually very cooperative and easy for the staff to help.

A common attitude among the remaining three categories is satisfaction about everything in their life except the fact that they have no place to live. When they come to the shelter, with a place to live and food to eat, they are satisfied for the moment. It came as a shock to me that these people were not really interested in changing the way they lived their lives. Now that they had shelter, a lot of them were satisfied to live the way they had been living. I know that people don't like to change, but if the homeless person doesn't change the basis with which he or she makes decisions, he/she is going to end up at the same place after leaving the shelter—homeless and broke. A lot of the people who are homeless have an income, and if it is a disability income, they fear losing it if they work. In any case, these categories of homeless are not particularly interested in work when they first come to the shelter. Some of them can't hold a job even if they can find one. To some, being homeless is so traumatic that they need time to get over the shock.

The third category, the addict, either drug or alcohol or both, is the most difficult and challenging of the homeless types, especially in a shelter which also houses families with children. They must at least get control of their addiction temporarily or they can't be allowed to stay. If the staff can convince them that life can be better sober, there is a chance that the staff can help them get back on their feet.

The fourth category, those with mental issues, can be helped if they can be convinced to use the mental health counselors provided by the public health system and they willingly take their medicine. When this happens, and it usually does, they can become contributing citizens and get back on their feet.

Unfortunately, if they haven't changed their attitude toward their affliction when they leave, they will fall back into their old routine, stop taking their medicine, stop seeing their therapist, and end up back in the shelter in a few months.

The fifth category is the heartbreaker. For many reasons our society has no facilities for these people. They are harmless and helpless. They do not have the education or the mental capacity to take care of themselves, yet there is no place for them to go. The shelter tries to help them for as long as they can, then they have to ask them to leave.

The staff's job is to help the shelter guests in each of these categories to get back on their feet. Since each guest has to be handled differently, the staff is always looking for new ways to approach the problem of motivation. The typical suggestion by most people who aren't involved in the problem is to find some way to force them to go to work. This usually means that they should be threatened with removal from the shelter. I disapprove of this approach because it is essentially giving up on the homeless person. It is becoming more and more evident that coercion is counter productive as a way to motivate these people, so the staff continues to try other means of motivation.

There are a lot of common characteristics of the homeless in the last three categories. They have very little money, no job, a poor self-image, and little or no self-discipline. Typically, they didn't graduate from high school, grew up in dysfunctional homes, and live by a different moral code. Most have lived in poverty most of their lives. Although most of the homeless are easy to get along with, they are very hard to get to know. They are usually hesitant to reveal the facts of their lives, so nothing that they say can be taken as the truth. Uncomfortable with rules, those who stay put up with these restrictions only to the extent necessary to keep them from being asked to leave.

The homeless described above have been given very little if any direction to their lives. In most cases the lack of self-discipline is their most important characteristic. It is a characteristic that **must** be corrected if they are to become economically stable. It is not unusual to find that they come from dysfunctional families and have never had anyone who cared what they did or who gave any direction to their lives, so they live by the principle, "if it feels good, do it." Largely due to their family background, they do not recognize the customs or mores that most of society lives by and that is a big contributing factor in the general public's attitude toward them. The resultant "bad" behavior has gotten them rejected by all the other members of their family. One of the ways that the staff of the shelter tries to help is to assist in getting them re-connected with some member of the family. If the resident is willing to change and demonstrates that he/she is actually changing, when a family member sees that the homeless person is trying to change, often that member will be encouraging, and, with time will take them back.

Unfortunately, society has developed a stereotype image of a homeless person. The poverty-stricken are for the most part outcasts in our society, considered either lazy and irresponsible, or dangerous, or both. For many people the resulting fear is strong enough to keep them from coming near the shelter to help. The picture of the homeless person that most people carry around in their mind is that of the panhandler you see on the streets in the cities. Rather than the stereotype, I suggest that you carry this picture in your mind. A mother and two young grade school aged girls were in the shelter one time for about 3 months. The Father had been jailed on a drug charge, so he lost his job, and as a result, his house. The shelter staff encouraged the mother to get a job herself. She then enrolled in the local branch of a university. She spent any other time she had helping the girls with their homework. When her husband was released from jail, she had saved enough money that they could rent a house and start over. She has continued her education and the family is doing well now. Although this image is somewhat ideal it is much closer to the typical homeless person than the image of the panhandler.

Another example of what the homeless are like is the first homeless person to come to the shelter the day it opened. This was another person sent to us by God. When the shelter opened, the first resident was a middle-aged man from Florida, who had come to town to be near an aging mother. He was almost a composite of the second and third types of homeless persons described above. He had worked construction until the job ended with the cold weather. Because of restrictions at her residence, he couldn't stay with his mother so he came to the shelter. As soon as he was settled he asked the director if there was anything he could do to help. He said he could fix anything, and it turned out he could. Since the shelter had just opened that day, the director gave him the toolbox and a list of things that needed to be done. The man went to work on the list and got them all done. Within a few weeks we realized we needed another staff member that we hadn't thought of—a live-in house manager. We gave the job to this man. I think God knew that we would need a house manager even though we didn't. Since our new house manager had a lot of experience as a 'street' person (he was also an alcoholic), he was street-wise and knew when the residents were trying to get away with things that violated the rules. He turned out to be a natural leader for the homeless culture. The other residents recognized that and did what he told them to do. Since we now had a staff person that lived in the shelter, we didn't need the security firm, and that saved us the money that more than paid the small salary that the house manager was paid. He made a great contribution to the early success of the shelter. Unfortunately, the job, the way we set it up, had a lot of disadvantages. He was essentially at work 24 hours a day, seven days a week, because he lived in the shelter. Being otherwise homeless, he had nowhere else to go that would let him get away from the job. The first manager stayed on the job for about a year, then left. By that time he had saved a little money, he got an apartment and another job. We found some ways to make the job less stressful when we hired his replacement.

Mission

I mentioned earlier that self-discipline is a characteristic that most of the homeless are lacking. I look at self-discipline as a spiritual issue and another reason that the churches should be interested in working on the homeless problem. For churches interested in mission work, this is an opportunity in your own home town. You don't need to go to another country to bring Christ to someone in need of him; instead of crossing the ocean, just cross the street. If there ever was a group of people that needed to be evangelized, it is the homeless. Even those who belong to and attend churches have very little self-discipline largely because the churches do not try to teach it. The shelter Board of Trustees would have liked one of the churches to step forward and conduct an ongoing Bible study at the shelter, but this has not happened, probably because none of the pastors has the time, or possibly because God doesn't want it to happen. Bible study is not what this group needs nearly as much as exercises that teach them what spirituality is and what its advantages are. By this I mean teaching people who God is and how he operates and what he wants from us humans.

Ambition and self-discipline go hand in hand, and with no ambition the homeless have few if any options for improvement of their economic condition. That leads to hopelessness—another spiritual issue. Even though one of our staff is an ordained minister, who holds periodic church services in the shelter, these services do not necessarily concentrate on spirituality issues. Because the shelter gets part of its operating money from a government grant, we cannot require the residents to participate in religious activities or such a program as teaching about God, but we can encourage it. Concentrating on spiritual issues does not necessarily mean Bible study. Too often Bible studies emphasize morality issues rather than spirituality issues. One reason that the government can never solve the homeless problem is that it cannot, legally, address a spiritual problem. It is up to those who get the money to encourage and teach the homeless what God is all about. The church needs to actively address the spiritual nature of the problem, not only of homelessness, but also of poverty in general. That is why I think it is an excellent opportunity for mission work. Approaching the problem as an economic issue or even a moral issue completely misses the point and will never change the situation. Teaching them about grace and forgiveness is a more likely path to success, in my opinion. The shelter has been open for several years now, and there are dozens of churches involved in one way or another, but as yet, not one has seen the mission opportunity and responded to it. Knowing God's involvement in establishing and operating the shelter, I can't believe that he doesn't want the churches to use this as a mission opportunity. I can only conclude that the churches aren't listening.

A lot of individuals in the community have been listening and are responding as their talents allow. These are the volunteers that share their talents with both residents and, in some cases, with former residents, who occasionally find themselves in need of help. They help by supplying meals, transportation, hair cuts, sewing and mending, teaching, and in many other ways trying to encourage those in need.

Chapter 5

Come, O blessed of my father,
Inherit the kingdom prepared for you
From the foundation of the world
For I was hungry and you gave me food
Matthew 25:34-35 (Revised Standard Version)

Feeding the Hungry

The success of the shelter should have brought with it a desire on the part of the evangelism committee to start a campaign of some sort to take advantage of the parish's participation in the project. This could have been an opportunity to promote the parish and try to get new members. Three members of the parish were on the Board of Trustees and several more had helped set it up. The shelter and the parish were getting favorable publicity from both the local newspaper and radio, but no attempt to grow in size was made. Instead, they turned their attention to the little emergency food pantry inside the open front door. By this point, the shelves were empty almost every day. Those who had been working with the project felt that more needed to be done in the community to alleviate a hunger problem..

The group that had been keeping the emergency pantry stocked suggested that the parish establish a pantry similar to pantries other churches in the community had, from which they could distribute food once a month, in addition to the emergency pantry. There were several other churches in the community who operated pantries, some by appointment only and others on a regular schedule, usually once a month; some had been in operation for several years. Maybe there was need for another pantry. God was speaking again, and he had gotten the attention of this group, so now they joined the others in the community who already recognized the hunger problem and were trying to do what they could about it. God does not coerce us to do what he wants done. He just suggests, offers, and waits for us to accept his offer, both in our lives and in solving problems. In this case God had been building up this group for a couple of years.

The way the churches supplied their pantries was to have the congregation bring in canned goods or boxed food that is imperishable, then on a given day, distributes the food to those who could come and get it. Members of other churches that had food pantries told the parish group that they could expect 50 to 100 people once the word got out that a pantry was open. It was questionable whether this small parish could afford to supply food for 100 people once a month following that method. It is a certainty that the hunger problem in a community of 40,000 people cannot be solved using this method, but no one knew that at this time.

Throughout the country there are regional food banks that collect food from various sources, including the agriculture departments of both state and federal governments, and distribute it through local pantries, to those at or below the poverty level at a cost far below the retail cost of the food. These food banks raise their own funds and buy food, probably from the food processors or work to have it donated from the processors, from retail chains, and from individuals. They distribute millions of pounds of food to the needy through local pantries. The parish investigated using the regional food bank as a source for food.

The food bank was very encouraging and invited a group from the parish to come to their facility for training. The training consists of learning the rules by which the food banks operate and by which the pantries they supply must operate. None of the food distributed by the food bank may be resold or used as payment for work done. It can only be given away to people whose family income is below a level set by the government. This level is dependant on the size of the family. Those who receive the food must sign a form stating that their income is below this level. The parish found out how easily and inexpensively it could get the food it needed to operate a small pantry. They also found out that they could not use the food bank to get food for the small pantry inside the front door. Since no one ever saw who took the food, there was no way to insure that the recipient would sign the papers to verify that their income qualified them.

The parish decided to set up a once-a-month food pantry and see what would happen. The food bank recognized the parish as a food pantry, so once each month; someone would go to the food bank, which was an hour away, to get the food for the parish to distribute. Remarkably, none of the other churches were making use of the food bank.

The parish's food pantry went into operation in July of 2006. About 10 people volunteered to help with the distribution once each month. Sure enough, between 50 and 75 families came each month to get food. The participants really felt good after each distribution session. There is something about helping someone who needs help that makes you feel good. The whole congregation seemed to feel proud of their parish and the work that it was doing. There was a sense of excitement in the group;

the energy level of the parish increased and the "helping' group grew in numbers.

The group also came face to face with more of the poverty problem. Although most of these people were not homeless, their problems were very similar to the homeless, just not as economically severe. In other words, they still had a place to live, but the conditions that controlled their lives were the same as those of the homeless. They are where they are because of the decisions that they, themselves, have made or are making. The problem won't really get solved until we learn how to get these people to change the way they come to the decisions that they make—the same as the problem the homeless have.

Even using the food bank, the parish found that distributing food once each month was putting a lot of pressure on the budget. Food Banks carry food that ranges in cost from free to just below wholesale price. As with many other activities, with experience one learns how to operate a food pantry economically. When the parish began distributing food monthly their cost was about $5.00 per person, and they distributed 12 to 14 items of food each month. Volunteers pre-sacked the items in grocery bags, and then handed the bags to the people who came for food. They tried to strike a balance of healthy foods, but because there was no refrigeration or freezer equipment, they were very limited as to the meat or dairy products they could distribute. The popular foods were available, such as peanut butter and jelly, macaroni and cheese, spaghetti, canned vegetables and fruit. Most of these items, however, were the most expensive. Once in a while, one of these would be available at a very low cost, but since the parish had very little storage space to keep the food, only a limited amount of the inexpensive food could be purchased. We all began to see that a large food pantry had some great advantages, cost wise. A second disadvantage of pre-sacking the items is that the recipient got each item whether they were going to eat it or not.

Just as the parish became concerned that they would not be able to afford to keep the pantry going, another example of God providing presented itself. A friend of a member of the parish, who lived in New Jersey, wanted to see the parish continue the food pantry, and sent a check for $5000. The pantry was financed for at least another year! It was becoming apparent to more and more of the parish that God was blessing this outreach. Even more important it was gratifying that some of the shelter residents were helping with the food distribution.

Many of the residents, especially those with disabilities and much free time make themselves available for all sorts of volunteer jobs, especially for those organizations dealing with the poor. Those homeless with time on their hands are willing to do their part. In this way, they are giving back to the community and feel better about themselves. This kind of attitude made it easier for the community as a whole to help. Kindness helps generate more kindness and problems get solved. Once the inertia of beginning to give is overcome, this type of attitude becomes self-sustaining.

By the summer of 2007, the food pantry group realized that there were more people hungry in the town than were coming to the parish's food pantry. They became aware that a lot of the people coming to their pantry were also going to the other church pantries. In effect, these facilities were all serving the same people, and there was a feeling that many others were going hungry and not being helped. As it has turned out, this was definitely the case. The group also realized that large food pantries could operate at much less cost than small ones. Someone in the group got the **idea** that the hunger problem could be better handled if all the churches combined their resources and created one large community food pantry, a cooperative effort similar to the shelter. It had worked for the shelter; why not see if the whole body of Christ, working together, could eliminate the hunger problem in the community? God was in action again.

The parish took the problem of organizing all the pantries into one large facility to the Council of Churches and the council put together a committee of 10 people from 10 different churches or agencies to work on the problem. By January all the details of the joint venture had been worked out, a place to begin the operation had been secured, and enough money and food were available to begin the operation. The group became incorporated and was recognized by the IRS as a 501(c)(3) charitable organization. The Board of Directors was made up of representatives of the various churches supporting the project, as well as the United Way, and the Council of Churches. The effort to combat poverty was gaining momentum and more people were interested in helping. The local Salvation Army gave the group space in the basement of their building and the community food pantry began operation the last Friday in January 2008.

The original focus of the group was to stop the "pantry hoppers" from getting all the food but still provide food for those who needed it. There was a definite feeling that the existing system was being abused by a few! To alleviate this problem several rules were established that limited who could get food, how often, and how much. Instead of being open once each month as most of the church pantries had been, it was decided that the community pantry would be open every week on Friday morning. Each family, however, could only visit once each month, and only residents living in the communities that were supporting the pantry were eligible to shop there. Limits were also set on the amount of food each family could take. The importance of unconditional service was not recognized and we were to learn that these limits were counter-productive.

At the beginning of each distribution session, volunteers made up two types of sacks, one with family items and one with individual items. Each family got a family sack and one individual sack for every two people in the family. An individual sack typically contained 1 can of meat, 2 cans of soup, 1 can of fruit, 1 box of macaroni and cheese, 3 cans of vegetables, 1 can of beef ravioli, and 1 can of beans. The family sack typically contained 1 package of spaghetti, 1 can of spaghetti sauce, 1 jar of peanut butter, 1 jar of jelly, 2 packages of Ramen noodles, 1 bag of onions, 1 box of a desert, and 2 miscellaneous items. Using food bank prices, the cost of the food being distributed was $7.26 for each individual sack and $4.66 for each family sack. The volunteers distributing the food were from the churches involved in establishing the pantry. The first few weeks the pantry had 40 families come for food. That meant that between 150 and 200 families were getting food each month. Operating this way, the cost to the pantry per person fed was about $8.50 and depended on the resources available. As had happened with the shelter, the community's response was both surprising and encouraging. The needed food and finances came from a lot of unexpected sources. It didn't take long, however to figure out that feeding 200 families per month, the way the pantry was doing at the beginning, would require at least 6000 individual items of food to be donated every month and that this would be a terrible drain on the finances of the church members. The antry staff felt it was urgently necessary to educate the churches on the idea of using the food bank and having the congregations bring in money instead of food.

At first the churches still responded by bringing in food items as they had done with their own pantry. The churches also took turns providing the volunteers who distributed the food. Eight to ten members of a church would be at the pantry each Friday, so the leaders of the pantry project had the opportunity to educate members of each of the churches on the economics of providing food and the cost of getting food from the food bank as compared to the grocery store. Now there was more space to store food than was available to individual churches, so the group could buy 50 or 60 cases of an item when it was priced low at the food bank. For instance, a can of green beans at the grocery store would cost a person about 75 cents. The same can, at the food bank, might normally cost about 40 cents. But once in a while the food bank would have those same green beans at about 5 cents a can and the pantry would buy 60 cases or 120 dozen cans. The churches were encouraged to convince their membership to send the pantry the money it would take to buy the canned goods instead of contributing the food item itself. The pantry, by taking advantage of the special prices at the regional food bank, could get 10 to 20 times the amount of food for the money that the individuals were spending to bring food to the pantry. After a few months, this concept caught on and money came in faster than the pantry was spending it. As the number of people coming to the pantry increased, as it did almost every month, it was becoming obvious that the pantry would not be able to keep up with the demand using the old method of people bringing in food instead of money. The volunteers from each church could see the problem and see that what was needed was money, not food. Through the summer the pantry was serving 150 to 200 families per month, but using the food bank to supply the food kept the cost managable. In September there was a bad storm causing an extensive power outage and many people lost the food in their refrigerators and freezers. That month, the pantry provided food for 750 families. This volume was difficult to handle in the facility that the pantry was using and in the three hours the pantry was open and would not have been possible had the pantry not stopped pre-sacking the food. Instead, the food was set out on tables and those coming for food went past the tables and sacked their own food as they went.

When the pantry began getting food from the food bank, the volume was small enough that it could be delivered by pickup truck. By spring the pantry had to spend $50.00 to have the food delivered in a small box truck. Finally by fall it was paying $150.00 to have it delivered in a larger box truck. Throughout the spring and summer the pantry had received more money each month than it spent so it had enough in September to buy the food we needed to handle the increased volume. Although the number of people coming to the pantry declined in October, the average was still over 120 families per week, a volume that was very difficult to handle in the basement facility. In November the number of families that came to the pantry averaged 140 per week and the board of directors decided that the pantry had to be moved to a larger facility.

At the beginning of the year the food was packaged in large double thick paper bags by the volunteers. As the volume increased this became labor intensive, so the opened cases of food were put on tables and the customers went through the line and took the food themselves. The loaded sacks of food then had to be carried up the stairs and into the parking lot. Volunteers had to do the carrying for the elderly and some of the women and handicapped.

The number of churches supporting the community pantry grew and churches from the small towns surrounding the community also joined in supporting the pantry. As a result, the pantry board of directors decided that anyone living in those towns supporting the pantry could also come to the pantry to get food.

The leaders of the pantry located a much larger facility on ground level, a building that had originally been the warehouse of a supermarket. In December 2008 the pantry moved to the new facility. In the new facility it was possible to place the food on skids on the floor and let the customers pick what they wanted. It was also possible for the customers to use shopping carts to gather their food, reducing the need for volunteers to carry the food out of the building. Also the truck could be unloaded with a pallet lifter rather than by hand, case by case. Space was now available for refrigerators and/or freezers. Four home-style freezers were donated. The pantry was then able to buy fresh and frozen food, which meant that they could have meat and frozen prepared dinners to distribute. Space was also available to buy even larger quantities of food at one time when the food bank had an item on special. The pantry started buying the maximum number of cases of food allowed by the food bank—160 cases per month. In December an average of 150 families per week came to the pantry for food. The staff began keeping track of the cost of food per individual served. It was $5.59 that month.

In one year, the pantry had gone from distributing about 6000 pounds of food per month at the beginning to distributing 29,000 pounds of food per month. The number of people served had gone from130 families per month in January to 450 families per month in December, and the bank account had gone from nothing to $9600.00. The community food pantry was about to take on an entirely new look.

What started out as a small individual food pantry feeding 50 to 75 families 2 or 3 days food each month, had grown to a pantry serving 150 families each week and giving them enough food to last a week. The ability to do this came from the churches pooling their talent and resources to try to help with the problem. The group could now see that they had stumbled (or been guided) onto what could become the solution to the hunger problem, not just helping with the problem.

When the pantry moved to the new and larger facility the newspaper and the radio stations in town all gave it positive publicity. This, of course, increased the number of people coming to the pantry, so the management decided to have it open two days each week. The newspaper's feature writer did a front-page story about the pantry and how it had expanded its services and reduced the cost per person of the food being distributed. The publicity generated donations from organizations and businesses in the community and from government sources. In January 2009, its second month in the new facility, the pantry distributed over 65,000 pounds of food to 974 families at a cost of about $12,000. This could never have been done in the original building, and was a far cry from what the individual churches had been doing only a year previous. The treasurer of the pantry organization felt that the pantry could not continue to operate at that volume, but there was more money donated that month than was spent. God does provide when you are doing what God wants done. The pantry expanded its stock to 25 items and allowed each family to come twice each month. The cost per person fell to less than $2.50, and occasionally, to less than $2.00. Mathematically, this doesn't make sense. The explanation involves learning to be better shoppers on the part of the pantry management, and getting the customers to take only those items that they were going to use. We were also taking advantage of the ability to buy big quantities when the price was low. By letting them come twice a month, the customers weren't as likely to "stock up" just in case.

As the economy worsened in 2009, the traffic at the pantry rose to an average of 250 families per week. It was now open two days per week, Thursday night as well as Friday morning, and the volume of food distributed each week rose to between 12,000 and 15,000 pounds, depending on the weight of the available items. The management of the food bank told the pantry leadership that most weeks the pantry got more food than any other food pantry in the region. The amount of money contributed kept pace with the demand, again proving that when the churches are doing God's work, God will provide.

As the operation progressed and grew, it was necessary to accumulate equipment as well as inventory. A foundation in the community donated enough money that the pantry was able to buy three new 45-cubic-foot commercial freezers and two 45-cubic—foot commercial refrigerators. By keeping the public informed of the operation through newspaper and radio articles, the equipment needed, or the money to buy the equipment, was supplied.

A couple of businesses in the community that had trucks operating throughout the state volunteered to bring the weekly order of food from the food bank to the pantry facility, relieving the pantry of the cost of transportation which had been about $150.00 per week. Food came into the pantry from sources other than the food bank, also. Trucking companies that had food they couldn't deliver would bring it to the pantry; sometimes bringing such a large quantity that the pantry had to share it with the homeless shelter and the battered women's shelter, or take it to pantries in other communities in the county.

There is no longer any reason for anyone in the community to go hungry. The food and the volunteers to distribute it are available in abundance. Not only have the money and food resources been plentiful, but also on the average, there are about 30 volunteers at the pantry every day that it is open, and an adequate staff of volunteers that come each week to unload the truck. The panty operation is done entirely by volunteers. Some are people that are getting food from the pantry and some are from the homeless shelter. The homeless don't need to get food from the pantry because the shelter provides it for them but they come anyway to repay the community for what it is doing for them. It is a truly community wide effort.

When people get food from the pantry they have to sign and date a piece of paper verifying that their income is below the maximum level for getting food. This is a requirement of the food bank. Using those records for the first 3 months of 2009, the staff found that the pantry had supplied food to 1256 different families during that time. 200 of those families had only come to the pantry in January, 200 more had only come in February, and little over 200 had only come in March. During that 3-month period a family could have gotten food at the pantry 6 times. Only 30 families came to the pantry all 6 of those times. The study was done to see to what extent families were abusing the system. It was wonderful to learn that the system wasn't being abused. People were only using the pantry when they needed the food. In November of 2009 the Board changed the rules so that a person in the community could go to the pantry every week if he/she needed food. It was also noticeable that as the conditions that had originally been set on who could get food, how often, and how much were relaxed or eliminated, the cost per person of delivering the food decreased. The Board was gradually moving toward the unconditional distribution of food to those who needed it.

It is clear to me through God's participation in the pantry effort that God is interested in everyone sharing in the plenty of God's world. The volunteers who make this pantry successful are merely being God's agents. It is through these agents that God's will is being done.

I feel that what this group of churches has done is show what the Body of Christ and a caring community can do when it decides to eliminate a problem. What has been done here can be done anywhere in this country when churches work together and decide to "just do it". God wants us to share with those who do not have. Scripture makes that very plain, and in this case, the abundance that has been supplied goes to show that God has blessed the effort.

"Bring the full tithe into the storehouse,

that there may be food in my house,

Test me in this," says the Lord Almighty,

"and see if I will not open the floodgates of heaven

and pour out so much blessing that you will not have room for it."

Malachi 3:10 (New International Version)

The week before Thanksgiving in 2009, I witnessed the fulfilling of Malachi's prophecy. There were about 20,000 pounds of food already in the food pantry when the food from the food bank was delivered. This time it came in a tractor-trailer from a local trucking company who had volunteered to bring 26,000 pounds of food from the food bank so that the pantry would be sure to have enough food for a Thanksgiving rush that was anticipated. When that truck was unloaded, the building was so full that the grocery carts that are used by the customers to get their food had to be moved out to the loading dock to make room for all the food. God had indeed poured out a blessing that overflowed the storage capacity and the pantry had the money to pay for it. It was good that the pantry had all that food because that week the expected Thanksgiving rush did occur, and 405 families came to the pantry for food. There was enough for all. The pantry staff felt that the numbers for 2009 were impressive—13,559 families representing 41,670 people received 760,585 pounds of food costing the pantry $87,395.32 or $2.10 per person served. A far cry from the problem as we saw it in 2007.

At the beginning of 2010 the volume of food delivered and the number of families served rose again. Over 400 families come each week for food and over 20,000 pounds is delivered by tractor-trailer each week. The amount of money donated to the pantry has increased a corresponding amount and the cost per person has dropped below $1.80. It has been amazing to watch. The average family gets between 50 and 60 pounds of food each week. They get between 20 and 25 different items that are well balanced between the food groups, including fresh fruit and vegetables and frozen meat. Even without food stamps, a family can live on what they can get each week from the pantry and the cost to the pantry is about $10 per person for a whole month's food. All of this is done in four hours each week. The pantry staff is able to put a family through the process every 30 seconds. **The hunger problem is solved**.

At the time of this writing, the volume of food purchased each week is between 25,000 and 30,000 pound and the number of families coming for food has reached 500. There is no reason for anyone in the county to go hungry anytime. The cost per person is now down to $1.20 for a week's food which means that the pantry can feed a person for less than $5.00 per month. God has blessed this effort as he promised through Malachi.

Chapter 6

Is not this the fast that I choose;
to loose the bonds of injustice,
to undo the thongs of the yoke,
to let the oppressed go free,
and to break every yoke?
Is it not to share your bread with the hungry,
and bring the homeless poor into your house;
when you see the naked, to cover them,
and not to hide yourself from your own kin?
Isaiah 58:6-7

The Second Shelter

Even though God had accomplished a lot through the parish, he was not finished yet. Their biggest lessons were still to come. What God had accomplished through the parish had not really caused any real inconvenience to anyone in the congregation. God

had gotten several people in the congregation more active, and had made them more aware of social responsibilities, but the majority of the congregation had been able to sit back and be observers. That was no longer going to be the case.

During its second full year of operations the homeless shelter was at capacity most of the time. When the space ran out, the staff started sending the next homeless person to the church with the `red doors' (the parish). They knew that the door to the church, which was only three blocks away, was always open, and they had been given permission to send the parish their overflow. God was about to open a whole new chapter in the life of the parish. The homeless who went to the church slept in the nave on the carpeted floor—not the most comfortable accommodations but at least they had a roof over their heads, and a place to keep their belongings safe. The shelter gave them a blanket and pillow to take with them. The parish became an emergency shelter simply because the front door was open and the parish was being hospitable. But, of course, this was not without its problems.

First the old controversy over unlocking the front door resurfaced. Now when a parish member came into the church, it was very likely a stranger would meet them and it was alarming and frightening. One morning the church secretary, who comes to work at 9 AM, went into the nave on an errand and discovered someone sleeping on the floor at the back of the nave. Alarmed, she quickly retreated to her office. I imagine that this reaction was more from surprise than from fear. But after several surprises like that it was time to review the open door policy. When changes of this magnitude occur our instinctive reaction to them seems to be to try to increase our security. This means that we put conditions on what we will permit and the way we will permit it. We as individuals or as a group withdraw inward and tend to rely on our own devices, limiting our ability to rely on an outside source for security. Our faith suffers at least a temporary setback. The vestry decided that they needed to put some time limits on when people could be in the nave of the church for shelter. They also decided that it was time to check with the insurance company again. The vestry found out that the insurance company's position was that the church was supposed to be a refuge in time of need, so the parish was simply fulfilling one of its traditional responsibilities. Briefly, that quieted the complaints because it made some people think about the reasons the church was there.

Up until this point, the parish thought that their hospitality was unconditional. As soon as a problem arose the unspoken conditions began to surface. Not all at once, though, and each different circumstance brought a new set of conditions. "These people who are homeless are not like us, and they frighten us", was the attitude that first surfaced. It was decided that from 9 PM until 7 AM the nave of the church could be used as a shelter, but the homeless had to be out by 7 AM. (Like the ostrich who sticks its head in the sand, if you don't see the problem it is easy to ignore it as if it didn't exist. The shelter informed homeless who came to the church of the time limits. Most of the time, the rule was followed. Usually any one person would be at the church only a few nights, by which time there would be room for them at the shelter. Usually, by the time any parish members got to know who was staying overnight, that person would be gone.

Then a second set of circumstances occurred. People who had been asked to leave the homeless shelter for reasons of their behavior came to the "red doors". Most of these people were alcoholics, drug addicts, or those with mental problems. This was a potentially dangerous situation, and danger brought out a second unspoken condition; the parish would need some additional rules. It should be noted again that even those who had been asked to leave the shelter obeyed the time limit rule for the most part. The vestry decided that the church would continue the ministry in spite of the few objections, but that they would also ask the shelter not to send anyone who was drunk or disorderly. A few rules were added to the list.

These rules, which were posted inside the front door, seemed to satisfy the congregation members and there were few complaints. Without any planning, the parish was embarking on another ministry to the poor, but largely because most of the congregation did not want to commit time to the project, it continued without any planning or direction. Some of the congregation were warming up to the idea of helping the homeless visitors when they could. As a result relationships were being formed which would eventually get those members more actively involved with the project. It seemed like everyone else in the parish had, on their own, decided to ignore what was happening so that they could avoid controversy. God was going to force the issue and make the parish recognize what it was doing and become part of the solution.

Frequently, now, there was more than one overnight visitor. At first this was considered part of the shelter ministry, of which the congregation approved and was actively supporting. God was ever so slowly acquainting them with people from a different culture. Since there were no incidents of anyone being harmed, some more parish members made attempts to get to know these overnight guests.

The homeless visitors were appreciative and most of the time they willingly obeyed the rules. When one of them flaunted the rule, the other visitors, themselves, let him/her know that they would not tolerate someone jeopardizing the hospitality of the church. This was another unexpected, but welcome set of circumstances. The visitors

themselves were policing the rules. This was a good development because no one in the parish was overseeing the project.

There were still those in the congregation who were fearful of the situation. Some who were against the policy from the onset found numerous things to criticize, and usually the visitors heard about it. The criticisms never received a voice, however, so they remain subliminal. Those who were in favor of being hospitable to the homeless were upset because the criticisms were a not a good example of the congregation's hospitality nor a good example of Christian love.. The overnight visitors endured the snubs and tried to be friendly, often thanking the members of the congregation who they knew for the privilege of staying there. Those who were doing the criticizing did not realize how unlike Christian behavior those criticisms were. In the Sermon on the Mount Jesus says, "Judge not, lest you be judged." Matthew 7:1. Luke 6:37 adds to the statement, making it more emphatic. The **statement** is unqualified and unconditional. A person cannot successfully minister to the homeless unless that person follows Matthew 7:1 100% of the time. Most of the criticisms and bad feelings that have occurred within the congregation occurred because someone was "judging" some facet of the character of one of the visitors. Good relationships are very hard to sustain when one of the parties judges the other. As I have mentioned before, it's very difficult to develop a good relationship with the homeless under the best of conditions because of their poor self-image. They generally feel inferior to anyone who is not homeless. They don't need judgmental criticism. It gives them a very poor example of Christian behavior. What they need more than anything else is to be accepted as a "person". Since they spend most of their time judging themselves, they need encouragement. From the beginning of the ministry, this behavior from people in the congregation was detrimental to everyone concerned, including the other members, as it was very divisive. At several points during the course of the development of the ministry some of the key supporters came close to leaving the church because of the unchristian behavior of a few of the members. Overcoming unchristian behavior is another reason that Christian Education is so important to the success of any project that deals with poverty. There will be more about that in chapter 8.

Another feature of this particular ministry that bothered some of the congregation was the appearance of the nave of the church. Under the back pews could be seen blanket rolls, pillows, and bags of personal belongings of the nocturnal visitors. Occasionally there was even the odor of dirty laundry near the back of the nave. To some this was like a badge of honor. It showed any visitors that we cared and were trying to help the needy. To others it was almost like a sacrilege. As time passed and more homeless came to the church, the blanket rolls, pillows and bags of personal belongings appeared under more of the pews. The feelings on both sides of the question got stronger. Those who were proud of the way the church looked started looking for a way to change the conditions so that those who were unhappy would feel better about the ministry, but no one could come up with an alternative. As long as the number of visitors stayed at 2 to 4 people, the situation was controllable, but eventually that, too would change.

Homeless people come in all sizes, shapes, and conditions. One of the hardest to deal with and help is the alcoholic. Since there are families with children in the shelter, drunkenness is tolerated on a very limited basis. If a person comes in drunk, and is quiet and goes right to bed he can stay, but if he gets unruly and threatening, he is asked to leave, and, if necessary, is escorted out by the police. Frequently, the drunk ends up at the church with the red doors. Since there was no supervision at the church at night, there was no one to talk to or get angry at, so the drunk usually ended up lying down and going to sleep. If he wouldn't and there were others there that he was disturbing, the other guests would ask him to leave, using the police again, if necessary.

Early in 2008, one such alcoholic, I will call him Ernie, a man of about 50, who had been at the shelter for months, came to the church. He was desperate and depressed. Although he had a job, most of his money went to child support, and after months of working and staying dry at the shelter, he had only saved a few hundred dollars. He could see that he would be years saving enough money to get out on his own again. To him there was no light at the end of the tunnel; in fact he was not sure that there was an end to the tunnel. His depression finally led him to drink again, which caused him to lose his job, which depressed him further. Finally, at the church he cried out for help. Up to that time, the parish had not experienced anything like this. They told him that he could stay until he got back on his feet, and that the church would help him do that as best they could. He could not find a job, but without money, he was sober most of the time. Street people, however, tend to stick together and reinforce each other's problems, so every once in a while, he would find a friend with enough money to buy them both some beer, and he would be drunk for a day or two until the money ran out. This pattern went on for most of the winter.

In March of 2008, just before the last winter snowstorm, another visitor showed up at the church, and his arrival changed the character of the ministry. I will call him Joe. He was quiet, thoughtful, broke, and admitted to a drinking problem. Joe had come to town because someone in Akron, where there was no room in any shelter, told him that there was a shelter in our town that was a nice place and would take him in. How Joe got to our town is unknown, but when he got there he found out that the shelter was full, so he was sent to the church with the red doors. For two days, he tried unsuccessfully to find a job. Then the snowstorm hit. He decided that the least he could do to show his appreciation for a place to stay was keep the sidewalks of the church clean. He talked Ernie into helping him shovel the snow off the sidewalks. When the storm ended a couple of days later, he noticed that the small paved parking lot beside the church was covered with 6 inches of ice, so they went to work clearing the ice off the parking lot. This got the attention of several members of the congregation, who made it a point to get to know Joe. A couple of days later, the pastor of the church went into the nave and discovered Joe sitting in a pew reading. As I mentioned earlier, the rules were that those spending the night were to leave the church at 7 AM. The pastor was disturbed that the rule was being violated, but a member of the congregation who happened to be there pointed out to him that the new visitor was reading the Bible. "Wasn't that why we had opened the door in the first place? ", he asked. The pastor agreed that it was a good point, and nothing more was said. Finally, the shelter had room for Joe, but he didn't want to leave the church. He felt that the church had become a part of him and that he was supposed to stay there. That was certainly different from anything the church had experienced up to that time. It occurred to me that we might be dealing with another person who was sent by God. (That's what happens when you start looking to see what God is doing in your life.)

The next thing he did was to look around the church to find something useful to do. He didn't have to look very hard before he found that the plaster in the nave was cracking, and separating from the base plaster. He found a member of the congregation and pointed out the problem, which up to that point, no one had noticed. He also told the member that not long

87

before he became homeless, he had had a business remodeling houses. He volunteered to fix the walls, knowing that when he was finished he would have to paint the entire inside of the church. The vestry decided to take him up on the project and supply the materials if he would do the work. He enlisted the aid of Ernie, who also happened to have experience as a painter and repairer of walls, and the two of them went to work. It took them a while, but in the end the inside of the church was completely refinished and looked beautiful.

Up to this point in time, access to the rest of the building, including the restrooms, had been denied to the nocturnal visitors, but to accomplish their repair work, the men had to have access to water and there was none in the nave or narthex or sanctuary. The door leading to the undercroft had to be opened, at least during the daytime. This meant that the men not only had access to a bathroom, but also to the kitchen, and this was to ignite another controversy. That controversy went on for most of the rest of the year, and at times got somewhat stormy.

In the summer of 2008 the shelter got more and more homeless and the waiting list got larger. The number of overnight visitors kept increasing, growing to six or eight regular visitors and every once in a while more. Joe decided that before everyone left the church for the day, the nave had to be cleaned up. He stowed all the bedding under the pews, vacuumed the entire nave and sanctuary, and even dusted the pews. The sexton was pleased because he no longer had to clean the main part of the church. Some of the congregation members were impressed and started taking more notice of Joe and the men who were staying. The visitors began coming to Sunday services and some of the other functions at the church. Slowly they were becoming members and their relationships with the other members of the congregation were growing closer. Criticism of the ministry within the congregation was becoming harder to sustain, as hospitality toward the homeless was becoming the norm in the congregation. But some of the neighbors were unhappy because of the number of unsavory looking characters hanging out around the front of the church. Some of them were afraid to walk past the church because of this.

Concern for the feelings of the parish's neighbors was a topic for discussion within the congregation. It was obvious that some of the neighbors did not want a homeless shelter in their neighborhood. I pointed out to the congregation that Jesus had something to say on the subject of neighbors. In the Gospel according to Luke beginning in chapter 10, verse 25, a lawyer asked Jesus, "and who is my neighbor?" Jesus told him the parable of the Good Samaritan, then asked him,"Which of these three, do you think, was a neighbor to the man who fell into the hands of the robbers?" The lawyer said, "The one who showed him mercy." Jesus said to him, "Go and do likewise." (Luke 10:36-37). I felt strongly that the parish was doing just that for the homeless who were our guests and our neighbors might learn this lesson from us.

The neighbor problem was serious enough that the vestry decided that it was time to treat the homeless as a more formal outreach ministry of the parish. Thus was born the "open door committee". It was originally composed of 6 members who had been actively involved with the homeless since the beginning. The committee began looking for ways to accommodate the complaints. They decided that one of the homeless should be on the committee and the logical person was Joe, because he had been there the longest, was attending services, and was taking charge of the visitors, assigning cleanup tasks and keeping the peace among them. The first project was to try to clean up the nave of the church. As long as the nave was being used to house the homeless there were very limited things that could be done, but Joe was up to the task. Every time that there was a special occasion in the parish, he saw to it that everything in the nave was cleaned—the pews were polished, the floor was cleaned even under the pews, the woodwork was dusted, the carpet swept and occasionally shampooed, the narthex was cleaned and the nave was deodorized. But there was no place to put the blankets, pillows, and personal belongings except under the pews so it was still obvious that the nave was a shelter.

Meetings were held with those who had complaints, and the committee tried to educate the opposition with some success, but traditions are hard to change and the tradition was that the church was not the place for a homeless shelter. On the other hand Jesus said, "inasmuch as you did it unto the least of these, you did it unto me." Many of the traditionalists weren't about to leave the church over the problem, but they would continue to campaign to find a solution without interfering with the church's homeless ministry. There were those who were equally adamant that the homeless ministry not be disturbed.

Finally an **idea** occurred to someone. Why not move the homeless to the undercroft? (How long God had been trying to get this idea across to someone, I have no idea, but I am convinced the idea was from God). The undercroft was never used at night. Occasionally there were meetings in the evening, but those meetings rarely lasted past 8 PM. The committee recommended moving the men who were staying at the church to the undercroft, and getting foam-filled sleeping pads for them to sleep on. The vestry approved of the move, so instead of using the front door to get into the church the homeless began using a side door that led to a stairway to the undercroft. This had the advantage that instead of the homeless congregating at the front of the church, they would congregate and smoke along the side and back, reducing the problem with the neighbors. The committee also got the homeless a refrigerator and a large cabinet in which they could store food. Because many of the men also volunteered at the food pantry they could get food to prepare their own meals. Arrangements were also made with the shelter to have one of the shelter's counselors meet with the homeless at the church once a week to see to it that they got whatever help they needed. A small room in the undercroft that had once been a small office but was no longer used for anything was made into a place for the homeless to store their belongings and their sleeping pads. With these changes the nave again began looking like a church should look and it smelled all right, too. The odor problem was transferred to the undercroft where it was more manageable and less of a problem. When women stayed at the church they slept in the nave, but their belongings and sleeping pads were kept in the undercroft, too. The congregation's hospitality was moving back toward being unconditional.

This change in arrangements corrected most of the complaints except the use of the kitchen, which may have been the reason no one suggested the move sooner. More members of the congregation could now see that what the parish was doing for the homeless was a good thing. As the number of homeless staying at the church kept going up, more of the congregation joined in the outreach project. More of the congregation asked to be part of the committee. God had moved the whole congregation completely into the problem of poverty. Since the winter of 2009 was now upon us, the committee decided that it was no longer necessary for the homeless to leave the church at any specific time, especially when the weather was bad. Another condition to the hospitality of the congregation had been eliminated. The controversy over the use of the kitchen was eventually resolved when a fire started in one of the gas fired ovens because one of the homeless was trying to broil a hamburger. It turned out that the oven hadn't been cleaned for a long time, was very greasy, and was not damaged. The homeless people cleaned the oven, several ladies in the congregation cleaned the kitchen, and the fire extinguishers were all renewed (the one in the kitchen hadn't worked when the fire broke out). Peace was restored when it was decided that the homeless could cook in the new microwave oven that was installed as a result of the incident.

An amazing transformation had occurred within the parish. It didn't happen in an instant, but slowly over a period of several years. A congregation who was more or less satisfied with the way things were had slowly changed, even though they thought they were not interested in change. God brought about the transformation slowly and over such a long period of time that most of the people didn't realize they were changing.

All this raises this question in my mind. Why all the controversy over trying to follow the scriptures and help the poor and indigent? The congregation had gone through each change and its resulting controversy unscathed. The changes had broadened the outlook of everyone involved with the project, homeless and congregation member alike. Evil had tried hard to cause problems and stop the parish's outreach to the poor and it had failed.

I firmly believe that the spiritual forces in this world had been battling over the
parish. There are both good and evil spirits at large around us. When God is successfully accomplishing a project the evil spirits become active in whatever people are vulnerable and try to destroy the project and the group where possible. Those

who don't believe in the spiritual forces, especially those of evil, are particularly vulnerable to this intrusion.

As C. S. Lewis points out in the preface to **The Screwtape Letters**, "There are two equal and opposite errors, into which our race can fall, about the devils. One is to disbelieve in their existence. The other is to believe, and to feel an excessive and unhealthy interest in them. They themselves are equally pleased by both errors and hail a materialist or a [2]magician with the same delight."[1] I believe that evil has learned to mask itself, so that we are unable to recognize it as evil when it is right in front of us. Evil has made us comfortable with the domination system that rules our lives. Evil finds ways to create controversy where there should be no controversy. Evil inhabits our churches and places doubts, fears, and uncertainties in the minds of faithful church people, distracting them from the task at hand when they are trying to be servants. Combating evil is a problem of discernment. Jesus was able to recognize evil and was able to expose it for what it was. I believe that our best chance to combat evil and overcome it is to follow Jesus' teaching. Of course this becomes another reason for an active Christian education program.

Compassion can contend with evil and win, but compassion must have its

weapons and they are found in the words of scripture, and in the word made Flesh, Jesus. Quoting from Isaiah, Paul advised the church in Corinth,

For it is written,
"I will destroy the wisdom of the wise,
and the cleverness of the clever I will thwart."
Where is the wise man?
Where is the scribe?

---

2 C. S. Lewis, Screwtape Letters

Where is the debater of this age?
Has not God made foolish the wisdom of the world?
For since, in the wisdom of God,
the world did not know God through wisdom
It pleased God through the folly of what we preach
To save those who believe.
For the Jews demand signs and Greeks seek wisdom,
But we preach Christ crucified,
A stumbling block to the Jews
And folly to the Gentiles,
but to those who are called, both Jews and Greeks,
Christ, the power of God and the wisdom of God.
For the foolishness of God is wiser than men,
And the weakness of God is stronger than men.
…Yet among the mature we do impart wisdom,
Although it is not a wisdom of this age
Or of the rulers of this age,
Who are doomed to pass away.
But we impart a secret and hidden wisdom of God…
1 Corinthians 1:19-25, 2:6-7 (Revised Standard Version)

I believe Paul's advice to the church in Corinth applies to the church in the U.S
today. We need to become much more familiar with the wisdom of God, which I think is what Jesus taught. Within the church, bible study should not be an option, but a duty, as members of Christ's body. I think that is the only way that evil can be overcome. Since most of the congregation did not attend any religious education, God was providing it to everyone with this ministry.

I believe the parish, by its responses to situations that God had presented it, had become sensitive to the social problems of the day. They were becoming more relevant. But now, what could they do to help those who were living in the church and very much needed help. They felt unequipped to deal with their visitors' problems. Several battles had been won, but the war was not over, nor had God's Christian Education class been completed.

Chapter 7

When a stranger sojourns with you in your land,
you shall not do him wrong.
The stranger who sojourns with you shall be to you as a
native among you,
and you shall love him as yourself;
for you were strangers in the land of Egypt."
Lev 19:33-34

The Grand Experiment

The principle criticism that remained in the parish was, "How long can they stay and do nothing to improve themselves?" There were those in the congregation who felt that the parish was enabling our homeless visitors to do nothing to improve their condition. The implication was that there should be a condition added to the hospitality that the homeless had to be doing something to change his/her status. Their argument went something like this. "If you had a warm place to stay and enough food to eat and no expenses for either, wouldn't you just sit around and do nothing?" The answer that most of the congregation had given was, "No, they wouldn't". That didn't answer the question about enabling, however. My understanding of enabling is when you do things that make it possible for another person to continue doing something that is not in his/her best interest. The parish was not doing anything for or with the people who were staying at the church. My experience has been that whether they are at the church or on the street, their actions are the same until they decide to change. Actually, in most cases, when they are at the church they watch their behavior more closely. Besides, none of the scriptures concerning hunger or homelessness put any conditions on helping them. In my opinion, the people who felt that way were trying to control the behavior of our guests instead of accepting them where they are. I will have more to say about that in the next chapter.

The parish was now faced with a critical problem as far as this ministry was concerned. There were some in the parish who wanted the visitors to either change or leave. Most of the congregation was opposed to that attitude but they did want the visitors to change. The parish needed to find ways to encourage them to change, however, no on in the parish had any ideas of how to do that. They thought it would be better for the visitors if they would change and become contributing citizens **like the rest of us.** The biggest problem with this approach is that the person changing has to decide how to change and they have to do it themselves. If a person is going to change that person has to decide how and when they are going to change. It also needs to be born in mind that change is not always for the better. Not to change is better than to change in the wrong direction. If we are going to get someone to change we have to convince that person that the change we are advocating is in his/her best interest. We may believe in the change we are advocating, but they will not do it until **they** believe it. One way to do that is to show them that the new way is a better way. We had a captive audience in the church with no restrictions on what we could do. Why not try to educate them? I felt very strongly that if we gave the people enough time some of them would start to change their way of living and making decisions and then we could help them. I didn't know how we would help them, but I felt that at the proper time I would know. Because very few in the parish were willing to exert an effort in this direction, my plan went into action by default.

I decided that it was time to give Christian Education a try. The church rarely had any events scheduled for Monday evening, and I had no Monday evening commitments, so, through Joe, I invited all our visitors to have dinner and discussion on Monday evenings from 6 to 8 PM. Since many of our visitors volunteer at the food pantry, they can get food just like anyone else. By pooling the food they get, we could have a nice dinner, and then discuss scriptural topics that might be germane to their problems. Not everyone was interested but enough were that it was a worth trying. The vestry approved of the project, so we started. I think that the idea would have been more effective if some other members of the congregation had participated, but no one did.

After a few weeks that seemed to be successful, I invited anyone from the shelter who was interested to join us and occasionally several have. We have had some people join us who are no longer homeless, but know the others who are participating and are still working on improving their own life. There is reason to hope that eventually, this project will show some success, but it is going to take time.

Joe had talked to me several times about establishing some kind of ministry of homeless to the homeless and poor. He felt that there was always a need in the community to help senior citizens with maintenance problems on their homes. He wanted to set up an organization that could train those who had no skill, or limited skill, to do the maintenance jobs that would let them improve people's property, while at the same time allowing the homeless to earn a little money. The idea was commendable, but he couldn't see a way to make it happen.

Early in the winter of 2009 an angry man came to the church with the red doors. I will call him Fred. At the time, the shelter was full with a waiting list, but this was the third time that he had come to the shelter. He was different from most homeless people in that he had a good education, had held responsible supervisory jobs, and was married, but separated, and had children. He had a drinking problem and that problem had cost him everything he had.

The first time he was in the shelter he was quiet and impressed me as being somber. Just by looking at him you could tell that he was angry. For a while he kept to himself. He got a job, and saved some money as all the people in the shelter do once they get a job. He spent a lot of time with a woman who was in the shelter. When they could afford it they got an apartment together and left.

After about six months, Fred was back at the shelter. Sure enough, the relationship hadn't worked out and he left. This time he said he had learned his lesson and he would pay attention to what our caseworkers advised him. For a while he was a model resident. He did so well, that when the house manager quit, he was given the job. He did the job well. Life became good for Fred, and he got careless and forgot about the lesson he had learned. He met another woman, quit his job at the shelter, got another job, and moved in with his new friend.

Early in that relationship, life again turned sour for Fred. He went back to drinking, and got caught trying to rob a store. He spent a year in prison, and then was paroled. When he got out, he came back to the shelter, then to the church with the red doors.

In the middle of the winter of 2009, Joe, Fred, and two other homeless men let it be known that they were interested in joining the church. All four of them had been raised in the Roman Catholic Church, but had not participated in the church since childhood. An enquirer's class was set up and they joined the class. They stayed with the class to the end, and joined the church in the spring. The people in the congregation who had actively supported the ministry to the homeless were very happy to see this turn of events because it represented real progress for these men to be trying to rebuild their lives. I also served to support the idea that what we were doing as a parish was a move in the right direction. It gave me confidence that God was behind my endeavors with the Monday night neeting.

In one of our Monday evening meetings we talked about the possibility of establishing some kind of a working ministry. At that meeting Fred became interested in what Joe was talking about. In the next few meetings we continued talking about a ministry along with discussions about how scripture could help these men change their lives. I suggested that they try to put on paper a short statement of what the mission of this ministry would be.

After a lot of discussion, writing and rewriting they came up with the following mission statement.

This is a ministry to the homeless and unemployed. The goal of the ministry is to provide employment and low cost housing in the
community. The ministry will help them by training or retraining
them in the skill necessary for the interior and exterior renovation of
foreclosed and/or abandoned homes.

Quite a few of the men staying at the church were interested. So they spent some time putting together a plan to accomplish the establishment of the ministry. Joe picked up a job in the neighborhood, which paid him several hundred dollars. He decided to put $250 in a bank account in the name of the "Red Door Ministries". The men made business cards and one-page flyers to advertise for work. For several weeks they tried unsuccessfully to pick up repair jobs. Finally they got connected with a local agency that had government funding to pay for repairs to the homes of disabled people or people who could not otherwise afford the repairs. The agency gave them a couple of small jobs to get them started. They also looked into the possibility of getting a grant from some charitable organization so that they could more quickly have the funds to buy the supplies they would need for these jobs.

One day a representative from a foundation that was founded by some retired businessmen for the purpose of helping homeless people start ministries such as this came to talk to them at the church. By the end of the meeting the representative told the men that he would recommend that the foundation grant them some money to get started. I have no idea how the foundation found out about our homeless people at the church. God had provided again. These men now have a new opportunity to not only help themselves to change their own lives, but to help others in the same situation get a fresh start and change their lives as well. It was exciting to watch this project develop. If we had put time limits on their stay at the church the ministry that these men are trying to develop would not have happened.

As with all other developments in this ministry, the "Red Door Ministries" project was not without controversy. There were a lot of objections to the name that the men had chosen for the project. There was fear that the name would give the church some liability with a project that they had no control over. Please notice that every time there has been controversy in this ministry, fear was what precipitated the controversy. That is why I have labeled fear as an instrument of evil. The vestry had several discussions about the situation before they decided, after the men described what they wanted to do with the ministry, to approve of the project as long as the church had no connection to the project. It was disappointing to me to see the congregation once again having difficulty with something new and different. The men, although discouraged at first because of the controversy, listened to what was going on, adjusted how they wanted to operate to quiet a few of the objections, and kept moving forward to get the project started. In the end it worked out that the vestry gave the project their blessing. As the winter of 2009-2010 approached the jobs available for them dwindled to nothing. At the same time, Fred's body started to deteriorate and he was hospitalized several times. Fred had been the energy behind keeping the others motivated and it was becoming obvious that he was no longer going to be physically able to do the labor type jobs that the ministry had been doing. God seems to have wanted the men to go in a different direction. Fred was finally reunited with his family and moved west. The "Red Door Ministries" is temporarily, at least, lying dormant in the background, but the men involved have also moved on and for the most part are at least no longer homeless.

One unexpected turn of events did occur though with the homeless ministry of the parish. Other churches in the community began contributing money to the open door project of the parish. They wanted to help the homeless, but were not yet ready to open up their buildings to house them. One church even volunteered to help with activities for those staying at the parish. Some very strong denominational barriers are being crossed by this cooperation and that is a good sign for both the community and the body of Christ. This turn of events was very encouraging for those in the parish who had been supportive of the project from the beginning. It had seemed that at every turn of events there was a new controversy, but here was one that everyone seemed happy about.

There have been those in the congregation who remained opoposed to the homeless ministry. Finally, after several congregational meetings in which the problems were discussed, it was decided to have a vote of the congregation on the issue of whether to continue or discontinue the ministry. The vote was a secret ballot in which every member had one vote, to be turned in by a certain time. About 40% voted and it was decided to continue the ministry by more than a two to one vote. It remains to be seen whether that ends the conflict or not.

As time has passed many of the people staying at the church have slowly changed the way they think and behave. A few have been able to get apartments and an income, so the assumption that given time, some of them would change for the better has turned out to be the case at least for those people. Whether it is the best way to go about rehabilitating these people remains to be seen, but there have been some successes and those successes have made the whole project worthwhile, in my opinion. An effort is being made to get some assistance from the staff of the homeless shelter, but as long as the homeless shelter is at capacity, the staff has a very limited amount of time to help

Chapter 8

Then I heard the voice of the Lord saying,
"Whom shall I send, and who will go for us?"
And I said, "Here am I, send me!"
Isaiah 6:8

What stands in the way?

I remember going to a workshop about outreach shortly after we had organized the committee that was working on establishing the shelter. It was a meeting where a lot of ideas were being grought up and discussed, so it was an interesting and informative meeting. One of the leaders from another parish asked the question, "What do you do when eople come to you at the church wanting help because they have no place to live?" What followed was a litany of excuses about why the problem could not be solved. Ouir group was in the early stages of answering that question, and we hadn't gotten very far along toward an answer, but the excuses got to me and I blurted out, "It seems simple to me. You put a roof over their heads." Fortunately for me at the time, they didn't ask for details of how they could do that. But here are some of the excuses I heard voiced.

1. Most of my parish isn't really interested in social problems
2. No one in my parish has the time to devote to big problems like that

3. We don't have much money, and projects like that cost a lot of money

4. I don't like to start something I might not be able to finish.

That first excuse sounds like me about 20 years ago. Two things changed my mind over a period of years—Christian education and God. The Christian education is what took the period of years. When I was ready, God changed my mind over night, but then I've already told you about that. I will have more to say about Christian education later in this chapter.

The time excuse is also a fraud. We are all too busy with unimportant things that we like to do but are not necessary or helpful to anyone. Before I got involved in all these projects I wasted more time than I have spent on any one of them. You might expect that the time commitment by the members of a congregation would be large to successfully carry out all these projects, but it turned out to be surprisingly small. The person organizing each of the projects had to make a substantial time commitment, but the helpers didn't. The little emergency food pantry inside the front door was kept supplied by spending an average of about one hour per day. Divided up among the members who participated in the project it averaged less that an hour per week.

Although getting the homeless shelter going was spread out over two and a half years, the time commitment during that period was not burdensome. The group met once a month for about two hours. In between meetings, committee members probably averaged about two hours per week gathering information and meeting with key people in the community or a sub-committee of the shelter committee. Since there were 11 churches involved, only a few people from any church needed to commit any time to the project. After the shelter opened, time commitments amounted to volunteering at the shelter for three or four hours per week if a person was so inclined, or preparing the evening meal once per month. Since the volunteers came from all over the community, only a few people from any church needed to make that commitment to make the shelter a success.

Operating their own monthly food pantry involved about ten people from the parish for about three hours each month and a commitment of about 8 hours per month for two people to get the food.

In the beginning, having homeless in the church didn't involve any time commitment on the part of anyone in the parish. When the number of people staying in the church grew, one of the homeless staying in the church accepted responsibility for keeping order, seeing that the rules were followed, and keeping the church clean. After the vestry formalized the project, ten to twelve members functioned as an oversight committee. They met periodically when there was an issue to be decided—about every six to eight weeks for about two hours.

When the community food pantry was started, the representative from the parish was involved in oversight of the panty as a volunteer, spending about eight hours per week on the project. The rest of the parish provided six to eight volunteers to help distribute the food three hours per month.

The time commitment, therefore, should not be an excuse to keep a congregation or community from carrying out any of these ministries. Spread out among sufficient volunteers, the time required, by any individual except the organizer, to keep these ministries operating is minimal. The thing that keeps a community or church from carrying out any of these ministries is finding a person or persons that are willing to commit a substantial amount of time to organizing and running them. Almost all the key people in both the major projects in our community are retired and enjoying life to the fullest largely because they are involved in the projects, some in both the pantry and the shelter. When the projects are ecumenical, the time commitment need not be a deterrent, because the human resources are very plentiful. It really boils down to what you want to do with your time. As Christians, I believe that we are called to tithe **both** our time **and** our money. A tithe of your time would be 16.5 hours per week. A small fraction of that by enough people would get any big project done.

What about the money? What about the cost of these ministries? Probably the most expensive project within the parish, from an individual perspective, is the little emergency food pantry inside the front door. It is expensive because individuals are buying the food at the grocery store that is being put on the shelves and the shelves have to be re-supplied frequently. It can easily cost a person $15 every time he/she fills the shelves, and that can mount up pretty quickly when it becomes a daily occurrence, and it will.

The community food pantry spends about $2000 per week on food and operating expenses combined, but divided up between 30 churches that cost amounts to less than $70 per week per church, or about 10 cents per day per church member if even only a small fraction of the membership contributes; and the community pantry feeds over 400 families per week. This is an expense that nearly anyone can afford.

Until the vestry moved the homeless at the parish to the undercroft, taking care of the homeless overflow from the shelter cost the parish nothing. When the homeless were moved to the undercroft the church bought them a used refrigerator and a cupboard in which to keep food, and foam filled mats to sleep on. Those items cost the church less than $700. The only additional cost was about a 20% increase in the cost of utilities.

The expensive project was the homeless shelter, itself. It operates on a budget of about $200,000 per year. Half of that money now comes from a federal grant. The balance comes from foundations, churches, individuals, and businesses. The county has a population of about 90,000 people. About 15% of the population has an income below the poverty level, but that leaves over 75,000 people from which to raise $100,000 per year. The shelter seldom has to conduct a campaign for funds. The money just comes in. Part of the secret of getting that to happen is, again, to make the projects ecumenical. Get all the churches in the community involved and there will be a minimal financial drain on any of them. As I have said many times before, God provides.

Does fear of failure keep communities from trying? Most people are limited by their fears. They don't attempt things that they might like to do because they think that they are too complicated, or they are too large an enterprise, or they are dangerous, or some other fear. Fear is a security issue and most of us are susceptible to some kind of fear. But fear is also a spiritual issue. In the Gospel stories, Jesus frequently reminds his disciples, when they are exhibiting a fear of one kind or another, "You of little faith". Fear paralyzes. It can keep a person or a group from trying something new. It can stop a going project dead in its tracks when it shows up. Fear of failure is a common fear, and fear of the unknown keeps people from changing and will insure that nothing new ever happens. Even fear that something bad **might** happen or that something **may** go wrong can stop a project from proceeding. I firmly believe that where fear raises its ugly head, there you will find evil spirits. And fear **will** raise its ugly head. Evil spirits seem to hate to see God succeed. Jesus was able to send evil spirits away through prayer, and so can we. Jesus equated fear with a lack of faith—faith that God will protect, that God will provide, that God will help. If we don't try to solve a problem because we are afraid of failing we are really saying that we don't believe that God can or will help us. So, it boils down to fear being a lack of faith in God. When we fear for our safety, as some in the parish did, we lack the faith that God will protect us. I believe that one of the ways that evil contributes to our problems in by pointing out to us all the reasons we have to be afraid. A major reason for the existence of the church is to help us increase our faith. Life can be free only when we have that faith that God is with us and whatever happens will be in our best interest. Most Christians believe that God is with us, but they find it too difficult to apply to their lives to put that kind of faith into action. I have found that failing to put full faith into action in my life kept me from living a full and active life for quite a while, but having finally put that kind of faith to work in my life has now made my life exciting and full and rewarding, and that is what Jesus was trying to tell us. Paying attention to what God is doing around you is a big help in building that faith.

There is a special fear that is often involved with outreach projects to the poor—fear of being taken advantage of. That fear was encountered all along the way at the parish. In every case, that fear was overcome eventually by getting those involved to realize that letting that fear participate in a decision was the same as limiting the project. The attitude that was developed throughout these projects was to leave that problem to God and move forward. There are those who will take advantage of every situation that they can and for the most part the only way to avoid them is to avoid everyone who has a problem. Scripture deplores that attitude, so leave those who would take advantage of us to God. In the end they are the ones who will miss out on life.

My experience of the past five years suggests that the main reason there is a lack of interest in alleviating the homelessness and hunger problems must fall on the leadership of the community. There are plenty of people that are interested in helping to alleviate the poverty problems of a community, but very few who are willing to make what they feel will be the large time commitment that running any of these ministries requires. Everyone has their own priorities of what they want to do with their free time, and for most people those priorities do not include dedicating large amounts of time to helping others. The churches, if they follow Jesus, are supposed to be developing people with a servant attitude.

Whoever wishes to be great among you must be your servant,

And whoever wishes to be first among you must be your slave;

Just as the Son of Man came to be served but to serve,

And to give his life a ransom for many

Matthew 20:26b-28

It doesn't take very many people with a servant attitude to accomplish large projects like these, so if the church leadership does its job the leadership will be there.

Once the leadership is in place it just becomes a matter of mobilizing that interest and that can easily be done if the churches work together and want to get something done. The best example that I can use to illustrate how to organize a project that can really solve a problem is the community food pantry (see chapter 5). When that pantry was organized we had no idea that it would become what it has become. A small committee was just trying to improve the community's reaction to a hunger problem. No one on the committee had any idea that the problem was as large as it turned out to be, nor did they feel that they could eliminate the problem. The committee committed itself just to try to reduce the hunger in the community. As the project moved ahead and got more involved some dropped out, but others stepped forward. The group took one problem at a time and found a solution to it, then moved on to the next problem. As the operation grew, from time to time a new person would step up and take on a segment of the operation. In the end, five people who were willing to do whatever it took to solve the hunger problem led the pantry organization to levels none of them dreamed possible. Those five people were from five different churches—four of them retired—they joined the group at different stages in the development of the pantry. All five of them recognized that God was providing the solutions; they were just his hands and feet. They were all willing to be servants and the problem has been solved without it being a burden to anyone of them. In fact, most of the time those five people are looking for other things that need to be done to make the operation run better and help more people. When we decided to start the homeless shelter, my partner and I had no trouble getting people from other churches to participate in the project. It was almost like they were waiting for someone to step forward and lead the effort. The same was true of the food pantry. Once the leadership stepped forward, there were volunteers galore to do the little bit of work that it took to make it a huge success. And some of them were willing to commit a large amount of time to making the ministry more effective. It makes me wonder how many other communities have people just waiting to serve but lacking that one person to step forward and lead the project. At both the homeless shelter and the community food pantry dozens of people stepped forward to help once the leadership was in place; and some of them were willing to devote a lot of time to making the projects a success. There is so much competition between denominations that most churches don't even consider asking other churches to join them in projects that are very worthy and needed. In most cases like that, the project never does get done.

We have a tendency to try to insure the success of a project by attempting to control whatever or whoever is involved. That is what was happening in the parish with the homeless people. Various members had their own ideas of how the homeless should respond to what the parish was trying to do. When the people a person is trying to control don't react the way he/she wants them to it leads to frustration and, eventually, anger on the part of the controller. There is a tendency to forget that God has his hand in the project, too, and if the leaders forget to look at what God is doing, they will inevitably try to control the results. At that point, their lack of faith becomes evident and the project is at risk. The food pantry faced this problem, too, early in its life. In this case we tried to insure that no one took unfair advantage of what we were doing by controlling how much, how often, and who could get food from the pantry. As we eliminated those controls the operation got more efficient and less expensive. Until we eliminated as many of those limitations as possible it was impossible to solve the hunger problem. Because we haven't found ways to remove most of the limitations that we have placed on caring for the homeless, we have met with limited success at the homeless shelter. Strive for the goal of **unconditional service.**

When anger enters the picture the project is in jeopardy. Jesus taught that anger was equivalent to murder. Anger destroys relationships and accomplishes nothing in the process. That is why it is equated with murder. By the time we reach adulthood we have, through personal experience, developed a set of beliefs and habits that more of less control what we do and how we react to the situations of life. If we want to grow and learn to handle life's problems, we have to be willing to modify those beliefs and habits as we learn what works and what doesn't work. Essentially, those people mired in poverty have been unwilling to change their habits when they find that they don't work. Anyone who works with this group is bound to become frustrated with them because very soon it becomes apparent what their problem is and you want them to change, rather than repeat the pattern that is holding them in their condition. That frustration can lead to anger and control issues, so the problem of anger can be expected to crop up early and often. It is very difficult to get those in poverty to change for a lot of very complex reasons, so patience is needed and must be developed when working with them. One way to avoid the problem, overcome the frustration, and develop patience is to develop a servant attitude, which, by the way, is also what Jesus taught. When I say servant attitude I mean learn how to give freely and unconditionally to the person or project you are working with or on and anger will stay pretty much out of the picture.

Throughout the Bible, but especially in the New Testament, there is a very prominent problem which Jesus encounters during his entire ministry and which the gospel writers all address constantly. That problem is the separation in Judaism of the righteous and the sinners. The Pharisees are constantly criticizing Jesus for socializing with tax collectors and sinners. Jesus had no tolerance at all for this attitude. His approach to the problem is very succinctly summarized by Luke in his Sermon on the Plain, (and by Matthew in his Sermon on the Mount)

Do not judge, and you will not be judged,
Do not condemn, and you will not be condemned.
Forgive, and you will be forgiven;

Give, and it will be given to you,
A good measure, pressed down, shaken together,
Running over, will be put in your lap;
For the measure you give
Will be the measure you get back.
Luke 6:37-38

When working with poverty problems a major problem comes from judging or condemning others. I cannot stress strong enough the danger to a project of people judging or condemning other people. By that I mean thinking in your own mind that the one you are working with is bad, wrong, stupid or any other adjective that makes them less of a person than you are. You cannot develop a good and helpful relationship with a person who you are condemning or judging The Gospels are full of stories in which one of the lessons concerns judging, yet we do it all the time. We have even gone so far as a culture to justify times when we say it is appropriate. Jesus, however, did not qualify his statement. His statement concerning judging is **unconditional** Judging others separates them from you and drives a wedge between the two of you that prevents the person being judged from accepting what you have to say. This is especially true if there is a certain amount of truth in the way you feel. People have to be accepted where they are before they will respond to changes that you want them to make.

Here's that word again—**unconditional.** It is a word that deserves further comment. What makes Jesus' teachings so difficult to follow is that most of them are unconditional. He doesn't give us circumstances under which any exceptions are permissible. In both the homeless projects and at the food pantry, we have found that the closer we come to unconditional, the smoother the operation runs. When we trust God and do not try to control the behavior of others we get more accomplished. When we put our own conditions on what we will do we are not going to be as effective. If there is concern that those receiving help are exploiting the generosity of the people doing the helping, the tendency is to try to eliminate the problem by putting conditions on the help that is being given. As I have said before, leave the problem of exploitation to God. Keep it between God and the exploiter Unconditional is a word that you **must** come to grips with if you want to develop a servant attitude. You must also come to grips with it if you want to be a true follower of Jesus. A true servant attitude cannot exist when there are conditions put on the service.

In one-way or another all the aforementioned obstacles are spiritual in nature. Dealing with spiritual problems is the business of the church, so it should present no problem for the church to overcome them. However, in my experience, a major problem that most churches have is dealing with the lack of spirituality in the persons of most of their congregations. A good adult Christian education program should be the answer to the spirituality challenge within the church but most adult Christian education programs that I am familiar with concentrate more on life after death than on life itself. We need the members of the churches to set examples of how to live and how to interact with people. The homeless people, especially, need examples to follow. Where else are they going to find them if not in church? How are our parishioners going to be that example if they aren't taught the basic axioms for living? Those who are going to be active in ministries of this type need to try especially hard to be those examples.

The spirituality problem to me is the biggest challenge the churches have. It is a problem because adult Christian education is not stressed enough in our churches. On a good Sunday, the parish will have 40 members at the worship services. On a good Sunday there will be 8 of those members in the adult Sunday school. The other 32 are not participating in the Christian Education program and most of the people who had difficulties with the ministry were in that group. If your church is interested in serving the poor, the place to start is with an adult Christian education program that concentrates on living, not as a preparation for dying. When the Christian education program concentrates on living, the members of the class will reach out, will direct their thoughts outside themselves and will start enjoying life more. They will be more likely to count their blessing than to worry about their problems. It will be easier for them to respond in a compassionate way to the situations that develop when faced with the problems of poverty.

Our culture has taught most of us how to live. We have learned the things that we should do and the things that are not acceptable. Most of these things approximate the teachings of Jesus. They are the lessons of "Cultural Christianity". Most of us have gotten very proficient at living by these rules and making our decisions based on the truth of these rules. We are not interested in turning our value system upside down. What needs to be gotten across to our congregations is the fact that these rules for living only go part way to being the truth. Christian education which concentrates on what Jesus taught will be teaching those in the class how to live. Jesus taught a radical way of living and in my opinion a much more satisfying way of living, but it is very different from what most of us are used to.

Not only did Jesus teach us how to live, he also taught us what God's principle concern for his world was To understand

Jesus, and have some idea of how he viewed life, we must try to understand the Hebrew Scriptures, especially the books of the prophets To view the prophetic books like Isaiah as predicting the birth and life of Jesus, as the Gospel writers emphasize, is to completely miss the point of their teaching. By getting a better idea of what the prophets were really talking about one gets a clearer idea of what Jesus was trying to teach. From the Gospels it seems quite clear to me that Jesus had a thorough understanding of the Hebrew Scriptures. Regardless of whom you think Jesus was or was not, He obviously had a very strong relationship with God. According to Mark, which scholars think was the earliest Gospel, Jesus began his ministry saying, "The time is fulfilled, and the kingdom of God has come near; repent, and believe in the good news." Jesus passion seems to have been proclaiming the advent of the Kingdom of God. Most of his parables involve descriptions of God's kingdom. By definition, the Kingdom of God is where and when God is in charge, and the powers of this world aren't. If the Christian Church is going to follow Jesus, then its principle concern should also be helping to bring about God's Kingdom. In God's kingdom God is concerned about justice. Scripture tells us what God's idea of justice is.

The cry of the Israelites has come to me;
I have also seen how the Egyptians oppress them.
So I am sending you to pharaoh to bring my people,
The Israelites, out of Egypt
Exodus 3:9-10

God's concern for the poor and oppressed was the main reason He brought the Israelites out of Egypt. Once He got them out of Egypt, He gave them a lot of time to think about how they should behave and how they should be governed. God's idea of justice included some economic principles. Leviticus

19:9-18 and 25:13-24 give you an idea of what God's view of the economics of justice is, and His solution to the problem of poverty. These verses refer to the jubilee year and to me they mean that God intends that no one can be completely dispossessed of sharing in God's plenty regardless of how he behaves or how little work he does. God has provided that they should be able to start over after fifty years. I doubt that these verses of scripture were ever lived as part of Jewish Law, but the intent of God is clear. Everyone was to share in the plenty of the earth to the extent that his needs were met.

When hundreds of years later, Judah was having grave international political problems, Isaiah, among others, came along to point out to the leaders of Judah, both political and religious, that their problems were due to the injustice of their actions.

When you stretch out your hands,
I will hide my eyes from you;
even though you make many prayers,
I will not listen;
your hands are full of blood.
Wash yourselves; make yourselves clean;
remove the evil of your doings from before my eyes;
cease to do evil,
learn to do good;
seek justice,
rescue the oppressed,
Defend the orphan,
plead for the widow.
Isaiah 1:15-1

Our culture has the view that a church's principle function is as a place where you go to worship God. A church should be much more than a place to worship on Sunday. In fact, what

Isaiah is saying in the passage cited above is that service to the poor and oppressed **is worship**. The whole first chapter of Isaiah is about what God considers worship. To Isaiah, worship was doing what God had ordained. This passage is not the only place in scripture where God shows his concern for the poor and oppressed. Justice for the poor and oppressed was a major concern for most of the prophets. .

Jesus, too, had strong criticisms of the religious leaders of his day.

"Woe to you, scribes and Pharisees, hypocrites!

For you tithe mint, dill, and cumin,

and have neglected the weightier matters of the law:

justice and mercy and faith.

It is these you aught to have practiced

without neglecting the others.

Matthew 23:23

Seldom, if ever, do you hear sermons on these passages. As long as passages such as these are relegated to secondary importance, the church will be open to accusations of hypocrisy, the poverty issues of our world will not be solved, and Christians will not be exposed to what Jesus viewed as life. To me, one solution is for the leadership to find ways to interest the members of their congregations to spend more time studying the scriptures, and to provide teachers who understand the scriptures and can present reasons why the prophets and Jesus taught the things that they taught. When this message gets across, even to one member of the community, the leadership will be there to carry out these projects

"And he (God) said, Go, and say to this people,

`Hear and hear, but do not understand;

see and see, but do not perceive.'

Make the heart of this people fat

And their ears heavy,
And shut their eyes;
Lest they see with their eyes,
and hear with their ears,
and understand with their hearts,
and turn and be healed
Isaiah 6:9-10

In chapter 13 of the Gospel of Matthew, the author has Jesus quoting the above

Passage as the reason he speaks to the people in parables. He is trying to get his disciples to understand what he is teaching. They often do not understand the significance of a story. Often, we have the same problem. It would be much simpler if there were agreement about the significance of scripture, but the differences in interpretation of scripture is a major problem for Christianity today. These disagreements are splintering the church and causing it to be ineffective. Historically, that has been the case with the church as an institution. It is important that we understand what Jesus is trying to get across and that God becomes real to us.

When God becomes real to us the matter of interpretation of scripture becomes almost a non-issue.

I will sprinkle clean water upon you,
and you will be clean from all your uncleannesses,
and from all your idols I will cleanse you.
A new heart I will give you,
and a new spirit I will put within you,
and I will remove from your body the heart of stone
and give you a heart of flesh.
I will put my spirit within you,
and make you follow my statutes
and be careful to observe my ordinances.
Ezekiel 36:25-27

Since God is not a material being—his presence cannot be detected by the senses—he tends to become out of sight, out of mind. Although you can't see God, you can observe what he does, or causes to be done. Only when a person becomes familiar enough with scripture to realize that what God wants is for each of us is to surrender our free will to him and follow him will God become real for that person. To me, this is what Jesus is saying when he mourns the plight of Jerusalem.

Jerusalem, Jerusalem, the city that kills the prophets
and stones those who are sent to it!
How often have I desired to gather your children together
as a hen gathers her brood under her wings,
and you were not willing!
Luke 13:34

When we are young, who God is, how he operates and what he wants from us is a mystery. As we gain life experiences, the meanings of scripture change and become clearer. We can begin to see what God is doing if we want to look, and I think that is the idea that Isaiah was trying to get across.

People get very little exposure to the teaching of Jesus unless they are involved in some sort of Christian education such as Sunday school or Bible study. A better idea of who God is and what he wants from the human race can be the result. The Old Testament writers described God by his works—by what they saw him doing in their lives. They felt that God could only be described in this way; therefore, they forbade any image of God. The same is still true, today. If you want to know who God is, look around you at the things God does every day. When you learn to do this, God can become real to you.

Here is an example of what I mean. Recently, we were redecorating the house manager's quarters at the homeless shelter. We were re-arranging the furniture for the family that was about to move in. When we were trying to figure out how to arrange the beds the staff person who was supervising commented that what we needed was a set of twin beds. Within minutes a van pulled into the parking lot pulling a trailer. On that trailer was a set of twin beds that the owner was donating to the shelter. The staff person and I looked at each other and just smiled. We decided that God agreed with her that what we needed was a pair of twin beds, so he sent them. What do you see in this story?

There was a time in my life when I thought I had learned all I needed to know about Christianity as a child at Sunday school. If I hadn't learned more about Christianity, as I grew older, I wouldn't belong to a church today. A big problem the churches have today is that many of their members are still living with what they learned as children in Sunday school, or what the culture has taught them. When I was a child I went to Sunday school because I had to, not because I was interested in the subject matter. I'm not implying that my attitude was typical, but I am saying that because of my lack of interest, I didn't learn much. I know that a lot of my friends were the same way, and most of us quit learning about Christianity as soon as we were allowed.

I did learn enough, though, to believe that Jesus had something to say to us. My problem was that I didn't see anyone in church or anywhere else that was living the way Jesus suggested. I learned enough that during my high school years when life got difficult I would go to the Gospels for suggestions of how to handle whatever problem was bothering me. During those years, I experimented with Jesus' advice. I found out that developing a servant attitude made me a lot of friends, and it made me a leader. When I was able to follow what Jesus taught it kept me out of trouble. It also gave me a lot of energy every time I helped someone else solve a problem. I became aware that what I was taught in Sunday school was a mixture of scripture and theology, and that the theology, for the most part, was relatively unimportant. Doing what Jesus said was where the power was. That attitude brought me into direct conflict with most of the "religious" people that I talked to and led to further confusion in my own mind. I did not know what God wanted me to do or believe. The multitude of denominations of the Christian Church contributes to this confusion because they each stress the importance of different things. As it turns out, no one knows specifically what God wants us to do in any given situation unless the spirit tells him.

By examining the ideas passing through your brain, I believe y0u can get a clue to what He wants, and to me that is what prayer is all about and that is how the spirit seems to work. When that is how you pray, you will find that all your prayers are immediately answered. There are a lot of different ways in which scripture is interpreted and understood. I cannot say what is the right way—there may be no **right** way. Scripture should help you manage life's problems and joys, the highs and the lows and everything in between. If the way you understand scripture isn't doing that for you, you should study it further. For a lot of people life is tolerable the way it is, so why go to all that trouble, why struggle with change? I will testify to the fact that life can be more than tolerable. Unfortunately, when the majority of the members of the congregation feel that life is good enough the way it is, getting Christian education of any kind going is a difficult chore and evangelism is even harder. But Jesus said something that gives everyone a reason to study the scriptures. As I mentioned before, he said. "The time is fulfilled and the kingdom of God has come near; repent, and believe in the good news."

Conclusion

Participating in all these projects at the parish has made me realize that God is continually active in our lives and will help us make our lives better if we pay attention. God can't help us if we don't recognize what God is doing in our lives and believe that he tries to communicate with us. I still try to figure out how I knew that God had visited me that night in 2003. Recently I found an interesting explanation of how God might possibly have communicated with the ancient prophets of Israel and Judah. A. J. Heschel[2], in his book "The Prophets" suggests this:

The unwilled nature of his experience is for the prophet part of his inner evidence that the message does not spring from his own heart.

But the prophet's sense of authenticity is more positive and emphatic than that. It is not the impact of an unknown, anonymous, mysterious incident, but a divine anthropotropism which he confronts.

The prophetic moment...was not experienced as the prophet's long-coveted opportunity to attain knowledge which is otherwise concealed. He does not seize the moment, he is seized by the moment.

The word disclosed is not offered as something which he might or might not appropriate according to his discretion, but is violently, powerfully urged upon him The impact of the anthropotropic event was reflected in the prophet's awareness of his being unable either to evade or to resist it.[3]

This description is very close to what I experienced. I think that part of the
reason I knew it was God who communicated with me is the emphatic way the message was received by me. That doesn't mean that all God's communications are that way, but it does confirm that God can communicate with us by putting thoughts in our mind. I have learned to pay attention to those thoughts.

The growth in numbers that was hoped for when the front door of the church was unlocked hasn't occurred. The few members of the homeless population who have joined the church have been offset by the older members who have passed on. The growth that has occurred has been in spirituality and faith in the membership of the congregation. Membership growth only occurs when the congregation invites people to join. The outreach of the parish did not automatically attract new members. It should also be noted that the emergency shelter in the church, did not take place without controversy within the congregation. Having homeless people involved risk for which some in the congregation were not prepared. Doing something new and untried generates controversy and criticism simply because of what it is—new and untried. It should be remembered that the homeless were not invited by anyone to stay at the church with the red doors. The parish just did not ask them to leave. It is my opinion that God sent them to the church. As with so many things that God does, there is a message there for those with eyes to see.

3 A. J. Heschel, *The Prophets,* p568

At the beginning of each of these projects there was little interest and excitement, but as they progressed both the interest and excitement grew and more people became involved. I believe this gives us a hint of what must happen for churches or any other group to get projects like these going. If a social service project is generally considered a good thing to do by the group, someone must decide that the project needs doing and start it. The large group won't participate until there is leadership to follow. Once the inertia is overcome, the public will join in and make it a success. Most people are busy enough that they aren't looking for something to do that is as difficult as getting a project started. They will, however, join a project that is well organized and going smoothly.

At the beginning of a project like these the likelihood of success can look pretty small. In the case of the homeless shelter, fear of failure was not an issue for me because I was convinced that the whole thing was God's idea and I really believed there was no chance of failure. I do think, though, that where fear of failure enters into the decision of starting a large outreach project like the homeless shelter or the food pantry there is a lack of faith that God will see the group through to a successful completion. That lack of faith has to be overcome. Any ministry involves risk and the more important the ministry the greater is the risk. Like Moses, we really don't want to be the one that God sends out to do his work. We need to have more people with the attitude of Isaiah—those who when God asks, "Who shall I send?" will answer, "Send me."

The members of the parish who participated in the emergency shelter in the church building itself found that by loving the homeless unconditionally, providing them with the bare necessities of life—shelter and food—, and teaching them "the way" of Jesus, some of the homeless began to change because they wanted to. The parish ignored the criticisms and just worked with the people who needed to change. At the shelter rules that are necessary for the safety of the families living there cause many of the homeless to leave, either because they don't like the rules or because they violate them and are asked to leave. When these people leave the shelter, the staff can no longer interact with them, so they cannot help them. At the church there is no staff, as such, and no families. We can get along with fewer rules and can tolerate behavior that is unacceptable at the shelter. Therefore, we have contact with them for a longer period of time, which gives us the possibility to have a more lasting effect on their lives.

To me the most important thing I have learned from these projects is **the Body of Christ can accomplish whatever God wants it to accomplish if it works as a unit and "listen to God.** Hopefully this story has given you a better idea of how God operates, that God is real, and that God accomplishes his will through human beings who "listen". In the parish's community the people from the various denominations of the Body of Christ that have participated in these projects have found that serving the poor, as Jesus taught was more important than their theological differences.

At both the homeless shelter and the food pantry, the Body of Christ has experienced and continues to experience the fulfilling of Malachi's prophecy. God continues to pour out such a blessing that it overflows our facilities. The people and the churches are learning from this experience that as a body they have the resources both in money and in manpower to comfort those in need.

Both the community and the parish have found that by becoming unconditional in their outreach they can serve more people for less money. By not being judgmental they have been able to demonstrate what Christianity **can mean**, especially to people who need understanding and encouragement. And they have learned that as long as they let God control the ministry the problems are few.

I hope that you will look at this story metaphorically. I define the metaphorical meaning as Marcus Borg[3] does in his book "Jesus"—the metaphorical meaning of language is its *more-than-literal, more-than-factual* meaning.

The homeless shelter has had a lot of successes and helped a lot of people get back on their feet economically, and in some cases, spiritually. The overflow shelter at the church has had a few successes, but their record is not as good. The food pantry has kept a lot of people from going hungry and helped a few in other ways, too. Those we are helping are not the only ones that have been benefitted. When I consider the hundreds of people who have contributed to all three of these projects, I think that by far the most people who have benefitted from the ministries and who have been changed are those people in the community who have helped make these projects successful. The community should be very proud of the work it has done, and the contribution so many of the people in the community have made.

Then there are the workers that organized and operate these ministries. I know that their lives have changed much more than either of the other groups. Most of these people are volunteers, but the blessings they have received are far more than any of them expected when they started working on the projects. They have seen what God can do first hand, and I am sure that it has changed their lives and their faith. They have benefitted in many ways that were unexpected; that is why they continue to work at the ministries. But by far, I have experienced the biggest change and the greatest benefits. My life has been completely changed. I am just not the man I was 7 years ago, and I

have never been happier or more at peace. Words are just not adequate to describe it.

Being a servant is, without a doubt, where the power is. The biggest benefit goes to the people who give the most, and I encourage you who are considering a project like this to keep that in mind. Yes, the people we are serving have the opportunity to benefit, and the benefit will be very worthwhile, but as so often happens in ministry, those doing the ministry end up being ministered to by angels and those to whom they are ministering

GOD HAS PROVIDED

Would you like to see your manuscript become a book?

If you are interested in becoming a PublishAmerica author, please submit your manuscript for possible publication to us at:

acquisitions@publishamerica.com

You may also mail in your manuscript to:

**PublishAmerica
PO Box 151
Frederick, MD 21705**

www.publishamerica.com

CPSIA information can be obtained at www.ICGtesting.com
Printed in the USA
LVOW10s1928130913

352391LV00001B/5/P